Dedicated to

Lori Peckham and the Brooks shoe company

So much happiness on this earth
depends on a loving spouse and comfortable shoes.

To order additional copies of:
Stop Laughing—I'm Trying to Make a Point,
by Kim Peckham, call **1-800-765-6955**.

Visit us at ***www.AutumnHousePublishing.com***
for information on other Autumn House® products.

Don't miss Kim Peckham's column in every issue of Women of
Spirit magazine. (You'll also enjoy the other inspiring,
life-changing articles and stories.) Subscribe online at
www.WomenofSpirit.com or by calling 1-800-765-6955.

Acknowledgments

Sometimes my motivations are not pure. I've been examining my reasons for releasing this book, and I find that they have a lot to do with greed and pride. Greed, because I want the money. Do you realize that Circuit City has a new gadget every single week? I'm trying to keep pace as a buyer, but it's not easy on my current salary.

Then there's the issue of personal pride. Publishing a book would be my greatest accomplishment since that time in Pathfinders when I collected pennies representing every year from 1909 to 1970.

Yes, we're talking about a real rocket boost for my self-esteem—which, frankly, could use a little pick-me-up after an incident in which I left the airport terminal without collecting all of my family's luggage. You would think that the three-hour drive back to the airport would have seemed shorter since I was engaged in the vigorous physical activity of banging my head on the steering wheel, but it didn't.

Of course, it would do even more for my pride if this was an *important* book. Have you ever read a book that changed the way you saw the world—that opened up new possibilities in your life? Well, this is not that kind of book. The only way this book will change your life is if you buy it with the money you should have spent on your heart medication.

However, it is my sincere hope that the questionable motivation behind this book will not prevent it from making some sort of contribution. Speaking of making a contribution—let me tell you how to send a donation to my PayPal account . . . Oh! Sorry. What I meant to say is "Let me recognize several people who contributed to this book."

There's Penny Estes Wheeler, who invited me to write an article for the first issue of *Women of Spirit*. Penny was my editor for the next 10 years and always had kind and encouraging words for me while she secretly searched for a replacement columnist who would turn in his work on time. Penny has nurtured a lot of Christian writers, and I feel privileged to be one of them.

Then there's Sheree Parris Nudd, who pointed out to me how easy it would be to publish this book. "You've already written it. All you have to do is put your columns together," she said, adding a "Duh!" for emphasis.*

Jeannette Johnson made the same point and helped open the way for

5

the book's publication (unless you found this unpublished manuscript in an attic somewhere). Also, I want to say something nice about the publisher, the Review and Herald Publishing Association, which has been my employer for a couple of decades and has been very kind to me, considering that they have very precise records of what I do on the Internet all day.

And finally there's my wife, Lori, who edits everything I write. If she laughed during the first read, it was a good day. But usually she would finish reading and say, "You've got a good start. Now why don't you try to put in something funny?"

Maybe you'll get lucky and find something funny in this book. And maybe you'll be doubly lucky and find something inspirational. Anyway, I hope you enjoy the book. It's time for me to tie this off and head to Circuit City.

---

*Actually, this book contains more than the *Women of Spirit* columns. It includes some articles that were published elsewhere and a couple chapters that are being published for the first time.

Contents

Take Control of Your Life
(or at Least Your Hair)

Admit it. You want to be in control. It's human nature. The struggle for control is the theme of every history book. First one person exercises control. Then—through violence or wicked scheming— another individual seizes control. This is especially true when it comes to the office thermostat.

Men, perhaps more than women, feel that everybody would be better off if they were put in charge. There isn't a guy alive who doesn't secretly believe that if he were made president for at least a week, he could straighten out all the nation's problems. Of course, this will be the same guy who has to ask his wife where he left his car keys.

Women, on the other hand, don't fantasize about controlling the destiny of 300 million Americans. They just want to control their hair. If a woman did become president, she would establish the National Institute of Hair and spend billions researching a hair spray that could hold every strand in place during a walk from the parking lot to the church lobby on a windy day. If she succeeded, a grateful nation would definitely put her face on a coin.

Women are also much more interested than men in controlling germs. It is an actual fact that a woman politician championed the law that says every public restroom in California must have disposable toilet seat covers.

Men have granted women dominion over hair and germs, but they would like to think they're in control of everything else. Everything, that is, except crabgrass, the stock market, what time the appliance repairman will show up, what the kids watch on TV, mosquitoes, medical costs, whether or not the computer will print, and the amount the car salesperson will give him on trade-in.

The truth is that guys don't get to control much of anything. Even a man with employees—who in theory must respond to his every wish— will find that in actual practice these employees regard his instructions with disdain and resentment because they are busy trying to auction office supplies on eBay.

9

Fortunately, God in His infinite compassion has given men two ways to feel in control. The first is the steering wheel. I'm not going to say anything more about a man's love for things with steering wheels except to say that if your sewing machine came equipped with one, you couldn't *stop* your husband from making new drapes for the living room.

The second is the TV remote. When I seize the remote, I become the supreme ruler of TV land. I can choose any programming I want. Notice how I can instantly flip from this advertisement for pickup trucks to this other channel, where, ah, they are advertising a sale on pickups, to this other channel, where they are also featuring an ad for some really tough pickup trucks.

Anyway, I'm holding tight to the remote. If I can control nothing else in this world, I can rule over those people who are flickering across the screen.

From history's point of view, the struggle for control continues. Yet I don't think heaven intends for it to be a struggle. Rather, it should be a great dance, where sometimes we lead by taking control of a situation, and sometimes we bow in submission as another takes the lead.

When we are at our best, we are like loyal princes and princesses, happy to give orders and happy to take orders, as long as it happens under the rule of our heavenly King.

It Is Not Good
That Man Should Eat Alone

Men don't eat well without supervision. Take my friend Chuck as an example. He's an intelligent, capable guy in every regard. Except that he has no clue how to feed himself.

If his wife goes anywhere, she has to leave him a bag of chips with detailed serving instructions. The refrigerator can be full—and he would still starve. It's like leaving a terrier alone with a case of Alpo and an electric can opener.

Oh, I admit that some of us can cook. But when we're alone, we get lazy. Before marriage, I never made salads because I couldn't face the grueling job of ripping lettuce leaves into bite-size pieces. Even peeling back the aluminum foil on a TV dinner seemed like too much effort. This is embarrassing to talk about, but once I tried to heat beans on a stove burner without taking them out of their original can. Now, that's lazy.

What guys need is a food that will climb up on the table under its own power, cover itself with gravy, and send an emergency broadcast over the TV that supper is served. Until then, most of us will just have to make due with breakfast cereal.

Let me just say that while I respect the men's ministry movement in the Christian church, no ministry to males can match the service provided by W. K. Kellogg when he invented cornflakes. The one recipe that every guy can remember is "Dump cereal in bowl. Add milk." As long as we don't need our wife to tell us where the spoons are, we're set.

My friend Richard is happy to eat cereal for breakfast, lunch, or supper if his wife isn't around. He passes on this helpful advice to other guys out there: "If you run out of cereal, just break up bread in your bowl and proceed as usual."

Men's efforts in the kitchen are handicapped by a lack of interest. We spend about as much time thinking about cooking as we worry over the colorfastness of rayon. That's because we have bigger concerns on our minds, such as how to get the song from *Star Trek* to play when we start up our computer.

Sadly, we don't even care about the healthfulness of food. Show a guy the new food pyramid chart and he'll say, "Hey, what's that? Looks like a big Dorito."

It's usually the women in our lives who encourage us to cut the fat, the cholesterol, and the sugar. Then the minute we men are out of town, they take off with their girlfriends to The Cheesecake Factory.

Which brings me to my next point. Women don't eat that well without supervision either. I admit that an all-girl outing at a restaurant usually gets off to a good start. Small salads will be ordered. The entree is usually no more than a baked potato.

Then the waiter brings out the dessert tray, and it's like something snaps. The same woman who insisted on low-fat salad dressing (on the side) is suddenly ordering a dessert carved out of a solid block of chocolate. Some of these desserts are so rich that they come with a coupon for $10 off on your next angioplasty.

I'm not judging this behavior as good or evil. The great controversy involves bigger issues than a slice of pecan pie. I'm just saying that we all seem to be better off when we have each other. Good company prevents the excesses that we might be prone to otherwise.

Maybe God was thinking along these lines when He gave us the church. Fellowship with wise and seasoned saints can keep us balanced—in more ways than just diet. Their influence can prevent us from binging on strange doctrines or unholy behavior. Because, whether or not we want to admit it, we all need a little supervision.

High-Mileage Relationships

In homes across this great country of ours, men are puzzling over the question: Why do women collect so many pairs of shoes? It's hard for guys to understand because we need only one pair with shoelaces and one without.

Well, the reason women buy so many shoes—as far as I can understand—is that shoes are for sale. The day that a woman can pass a display of shoes without picking one up is the day that I can walk by a box of warm Krispy Kreme donuts.

Now, in the interest of fair play, we will take a question from a woman in our audience. Yes, you in the teal suede pumps with eelskin detail. State your question.

"What's the deal with men and cars?"

Good question. Cars illustrate one difference between a man's relationships and a woman's. Women generally feel that if they are going to invest time and energy in a relationship, it should involve an actual human being. Men are not so picky.

We look at a car and say, "It's bright and shiny. It lets me be in total control *and* it doesn't talk much. This could be the start of something beautiful."

As time passes, we can become downright sentimental about our set of wheels. Burly men who jackhammer rocks for a living will dab at their eyes as they remember their first automobile.

My pastor admits to being so attached to a beat-up Toyota that he continued to drive it even when the only way into the car was through the hatchback. I've heard of men demanding to be buried in their cars, though a fellow will feel mighty silly when he wakes up on the resurrection day in a '76 Eldorado with a dead battery.

Men will shower a great deal of attention on cars. You should see the effort my cousin Dave puts into hand-waxing his van—a vehicle with nearly as much sheet metal as a grain barn.

Some men are also very protective, which explains the popularity of car alarms. Car alarms prevent theft by going off at random times throughout the night so that everyone in the neighborhood will be awake and alert to the presence of prowlers.

As my wife walked through a parking lot the other day, she was surprised by a car alarm that actually spoke to her. She had brushed past a pickup when an electronic voice growled, "Protected by Viper. Stand back."

While this might be the right thing to say to prevent theft, wouldn't it be more Christian to offer a word of encouragement to passersby? How much nicer if you were walking through a parking lot and heard, "You're looking good! Have you been working out?"

So why do guys like cars so much? It might have something to do with power and independence and ancestral memories of riding across the plains in a chariot. Or it might just be the comfort of six-way adjustable seats. I asked my dad—who is not usually the sentimental type—why he would never part with a '72 Ford he called "Old Blue."

"I don't know," he mused. "It's like a favorite horse. When he comes to the end of his career, you don't send him to the rendering plant."

I think Old Blue was my dad's favorite because he spent 286,000 miles in the driver's seat.

Given enough time, you can build a relationship with anybody or anything. Or to put it another way, it takes time to build a relationship.

So, are you spending enough time on your important relationships? I don't have any reason to believe you aren't, but if the shoe fits . . .

Percentage of American women who say their car is "more reliable" than most men they know: 49. *Harper's*

For Crying Out Loud!

The modern man: tough, yet tender. Strong when he needs to be, yet confident enough in his manhood to shed a tear at emotional moments. So far those moments have been limited to sudden reverses in the stock market and the final scenes of the movie *Babe*. But these are progressive times, and I'm personally looking forward to the day when men can cry to get themselves out of speeding tickets.

Meanwhile, women do most of the crying because they don't feel self-conscious about it. They treat it the same way that men treat a belch—it's something you apologize for, but not something you avoid. So it's not uncommon to see women crying in public. Especially coming out of the beauty salon with a new perm.

On the other hand, men don't want anyone to see them cry. You catch a guy with tears in his eyes, and he'll feel that he has no choice but to change his name and move to the Yukon. When a guy finds himself in the grip of a melancholy emotion, he starts tilting his head back ever so slightly and hopes that the tears will seep back under his eyeballs.

Men are afraid that crying will make them look weak and unstable. And it's true. You don't want to see the president of the country come on TV and start sobbing and saying how hard he has tried to be nice and get along with the Democratic Congress, but they just keep saying the most hurtful things behind his back and (sniff) he is at his wit's end.

Because of our inhibitions, we guys miss out on the comforting qualities of a good cry. Women have always found solace in sobs when faced with tragedies such as death, sickness, or stubborn laundry stains. Our friend Trish—a mother of two adult kids—cries to relieve the sense of loss when Frosty the Snowman melts at the end of the Christmas special.

Like I said, men miss out on comfort crying. And it just might be a change for the better if men reacted to a Super Bowl loss by flopping onto the bed and getting the pillows wet.

Men also lag behind women in crying for joy—you know, recre-

15

ational crying. Women quickly moisten their eyelashes at moments of great tenderness and beauty. These moments include the rebaptism of family members, touching Christmas stories, and Hallmark card commercials. If a woman says she cried when she watched a video, she is essentially giving it two thumbs-up.

It's this idea of weeping at moments of great beauty that makes me wonder if John the revelator got it right when he says God will wipe away every tear from our eyes. Of course, you don't need a lot of Kleenex if there is no pain, no sorrow, no goodbyes.

But the thing that gets me is a memory from my childhood. My dad would read to us kids out of Uncle Arthur's *The Bible Story*. And I remember that when he got to the story of Jesus on the cross, I looked up and saw tears in his eyes. I'd never seen that before, so it made an impression.

Myself, I don't usually cry upon hearing that story. I'm afraid I take it for granted. But when I'm standing on the Sea of Glass and the choir starts to sing, I can imagine that the beauty of the cross will hit me with the force of an ocean wave. And maybe—out of habit—I'll start tilting my head back ever so slightly.

Now You're Scaring Me

Worry is a part of life. Especially if you're a church greeter during cold and flu season.

Still, we worry too much. When I say this, I'm not talking to men who make a big show of not worrying about *anything*—until their wife leaves the house with the Bloomingdale's charge card. No, I am talking to women, who wear their anxiety right out where you can see it like a big corsage.

Men are always trying to soothe the unreasonable anxieties of women by saying, "Don't worry, honey. It doesn't look like a *poisonous* snake." Or "Don't worry, Mom. You'll be safe in that part of town as long as you don't make eye contact with anyone."

I want to urge women everywhere to try to relax, because when you're nervous, we're nervous. In particular, I'd like to mention a certain noise you make in times of consternation— the gasp.

My wife often chooses to use the gasp when we're driving peacefully down the road. There is something about that sound that shoots a quart of adrenaline into my bloodstream and causes me to veer into the oncoming traffic, figuring that death from collision is preferable to whatever terror brought forth that sound.

"What is it?" I shriek in panic. "What is it?"

She will turn to me, eyes wide with horror. "I forgot to send a birthday card to Aunt Elsie."

This brings me to one of the big problems with both the gasp and the scream. They convey no useful information. For example, the same scream can mean either "A strange man is coming at me with a butcher knife!" or "The cat is eating my breakfast cereal!" Sometimes it can even mean "Look over there! It's Barry Manilow!"

Men don't scream. Which is why the airlines have mostly male pilots. No one wants to be on a transcontinental flight and hear, "This is your captain speaking . . . AAEEEEEEEEE!" You can count on men to give you the facts with unruffled composure. "This is your captain speaking. Due to mechanical problems, we will be crashing south of Omaha. This means you will be awarded only half the frequent flyer miles that you expected for this flight."

Because women worry more, I think they take more precautions. Once, when my cousin Gina was home alone, a strange woman came to the door asking to use the phone. Gina took the precaution of getting a sharp knife and dramatically pealing a nectarine while the stranger made her call—Gina's way of letting the woman know that she better not try any funny stuff.

Our friend Patty took the precaution of naming her cat Henry. If she gets a suspicious phone call, she will warn the caller that she is not alone by yelling over her shoulder, "Henry! Would you see who's at the door?"

While it makes sense to take precautions, I still think we worry too much. Men worry about their job, politics, and getting a ding on their new car. Women worry about child kidnappers, germs, serial murderers, germs, children running with sharp sticks, and germs.

While it's completely natural to worry, I think God takes it as a compliment when we don't—when we trust Him so completely that our anxieties drain away and we're left with perfect peace.

Consider the lilies—how they never fret. Nor gasp.

Sick Behavior

It occurs to me that I haven't been to the dentist in a long while. He used to send me little postcard reminders: "It's been six months since your last checkup." Followed by "It's been two years since your last checkup." And finally, "We have filed a missing person's report with the local authorities."

The people at the dentist's office are nice enough. And they have this charming way of acting surprised when the process of stabbing my gums with sharp metal instruments draws blood. But I still can't get enthused about making an appointment. If I want pain, I'll watch a high school production of *Cats*.

My wife, on the other hand, loves visiting any health professional. Give her the choice between a CT scan and a trip to Cancún, and she'll have to think about it.

I think she enjoys visiting health professionals because they're more sympathetic than I am.

They will listen to her complaints for up to 10 minutes before looking at their watches. And, unlike me, they never interrupt her to ask what's for dinner.

It's not that I don't care about her well-being. I just want to see some concrete symptoms. If she changed color or something, then she'd get sympathy. But her symptoms always have an indefinite quality, like a funny noise in your car that disappears as soon as you hand the keys to a mechanic.

"Come listen to my heart," she'll say. "I think it's beating funny."

"Only if 60 beats a minute is funny," I'll respond.

In general, men may be a little slow to give sympathy, but we don't ask for a lot of it either. Men drive off to the office with a temperature of 105°, convinced that they can function even if they can't actually sit up in their chair without the aid of duct tape.

"I have to get to work," we whisper as we drag ourselves across the floor. "The place will come apart without me. I hate to think what will happen if I don't finish my report on company pencil usage."

We actually take offense when our wives suggest we see a doctor: "What exactly are you saying, dear? You think I'm not man enough to handle a little bout of Legionnaire's disease? I can shake this off."

The idea of going to a doctor insults our independence. It's like stopping the car to ask for directions. If physicians had to depend on male patients to make a living, you'd find them on street corners with a piece of cardboard strung around their neck that reads "Will diagnose for food."

All this makes me think that there's a huge market for do-it-yourself health care among men. Give guys a mirror and an exactoknife, and we'll try to extract our own tonsils. I know a guy who nonchalantly removed his facial mole with a pair of wire cutters.

Even so, men are not widely respected for their ability to handle pain. As my friend Olive says, "If it were up to men to give birth, the human race would have faded away long ago."

Men spurn sympathy until they reach a certain threshold of agony. Then we dissolve into megababies who curl up on the couch and quietly moan, "Why must the innocent suffer?" and "Will you bring me a Kool Pop?"

My buddy Larry likes to carry a Kleenex box around with him as a sort of sympathy magnet. Sometimes there is nothing more satisfying than someone saying, "You look awful."

I wonder why sympathy is so important to us. It doesn't take away the headache like Tylenol does. I suppose sympathy serves as a currency of love. Proof that someone cares.

And when we need proof that God cares, we can remember that He humbled Himself in human flesh. It's an enormous comfort to know that He has felt our infirmities. That He understands toothaches and sore feet and upset stomachs.

And, when sympathy isn't enough, we can remember that He's the physician, too.

Shop Till He Drops

Whoever said women are the weaker sex has never seen one shop. When I see my wife come out of the mall—sometimes days after she went in—I am awestruck by the display of human endurance. I've known men who have the stamina to run marathons, but ask one of them to look through 20 racks of spring dresses, and he will beg for mercy.

I speak from experience. When we first got married, I tried to go shopping with Lori. I thought it would be nice to share her hobbies. But after 10 minutes of watching her compare shades of panty hose, I thought, *Wait, I don't want to suffocate this relationship by constantly hovering over my wife. Perhaps it's best if I go somewhere and get a snack.*

There's something about the marble floors, the Muzak, and the dress racks stretching to the horizon that can make a man feel as out of place as a violinist at a biker barbeque. The people who build malls seem to consider men as one of those embarrassing facts of life that are best ignored—sort of like dandruff or Howard Stern. I mean, some stores have playrooms where you can drop off the kids. But there's no place where you can drop off the men.

Instead, you find them abandoned on benches next to the potted ferns, or loitering around the electronics department watching *Oprah*. There's something about the lonely, lost look in their eyes that reminds me of the refugee mailings from ADRA.

One of the reasons that men are so hopeless at shopping is that they don't have the patience to browse. Women resemble impalas, and the malls are their Serengeti Plain. They nibble here. They nibble there. The only difference is that the impala is not surrounded by sales associates offering to find the grass in the same color but a larger size.

When men shop, they don't graze their way through the aisles. They swoop down on their purchases like the noble eagle. My friend Mark once went into a store, bought two suits, had them fitted and accessorized with shirts and ties, and was on his way in 20 minutes.

It takes my wife that long just to find the right credit card.

I've given up shopping with Lori. So, she brings the shopping home to me. "Which shoes look best with this dress?" she'll ask.

Asking a man this question is about as likely to have a satisfactory result as asking a pet canary which word processing program it prefers.

Part of the problem is that a man looks at new clothes differently from a woman. She sees a silk pantsuit. The guy sees a house payment.

Over the years, I've tried to learn what to say when faced with a new outfit. Here's what I think works best:

a. . . .

Well, actually, I've had more experience with what *not* to say:

a. Don't you already own a dress?

b. Does the dollar store have a clothing line now?

c. Doesn't Barbara Bush have an outfit like that?

You have to understand that men are motivated to criticize a new outfit because if the woman takes it back, the man gets to keep the money for something *he* wants, such as new mud flaps for the pickup.

But criticizing clothes is a lot like taking Pathfinders to the beach: someone is bound to get burned. Shopping takes a lot of effort, and it hurts when the fruit of that effort is dismissed.

When the shoe is on the other foot and I buy an article of clothing for Lori, I want it to be like *Little House on the Prairie*. You know, the guy comes back from town with a few yards of calico, and the woman is so touched that big tears of gratitude drop onto the freshly swept dirt floor.

There's a lesson I've learned from this: It's easy—even tempting—to criticize the faults of the preacher, the special music, or the fifth-grade teacher. But gratitude for the good things people have to offer seems more helpful in the long run.

A few kind words, and the people who minister to us in the church will display an endurance that you don't see very often—at least outside of a mall.

"My Goat-haired, Wheat-bellied Baby"

We're going to talk about the Song of Solomon, a book that is so steamy I'm surprised it got in the Bible without a parental advisory sticker. So if you're under the age of 17 or were raised in the Midwest and taught that the only appropriate time to discuss sex is in the context of cattle breeding, then you might want to skip this article. Actually, I want to skip this article, because I was raised in Kansas. The only time I remember anyone talking about romance was when Nancy Van Pelt visited my academy.

But you haven't stopped reading (yet), so I won't stop writing. We're going to look to King Sol for some tips on how to communicate with our marriage partners. I assume we already know the importance of communication in a happy relationship (unless you've done something really stupid, such as trying to heat up a can of Yoo-Hoo in the microwave. Then the less said the better). OK, let's see what the wise one suggests we should say when we want to do a little wooing.

"I liken you, my darling, to a mare harnessed to one of the chariots of Pharaoh" (chapter 1, verse 9).

Apparently, Solomon has chosen to flatter the dark and lovely object of his affection by likening her to a horse. If you ask me, it's risky to compare a woman to any animal that weighs more than a thousand pounds. So if you're going to draw an analogy, pick a very small animal. "Kitten," "dove," and "paramecium" are all workable pet names.

Of course, who am I to second-guess the Bible's greatest romantic? The guy took more trips to the marriage altar than I've taken to Taco Bell.

"How beautiful you are, my darling! Oh, how beautiful! Your eyes are doves" (chapter 1, verse 15).

Notice how the king refers to his beloved as "beautiful" twice in the space of nine words. Sol is really onto something here. I've discovered that the secret of a happy marriage is to comment on my wife's surpassing beauty on the hour and the half hour—more often if I've just tracked mud onto the carpet.

"Like a lily among thorns is my darling among the maidens" (chapter 2, verse 2).

Another compliment! Keep in mind that compliments are cheap. You can call your beloved a lily and get almost as many points as if you bought a bouquet at the florist. Then you can use the money for something you *both* can use, such as a new chain saw.

"Your hair is like a flock of goats descending from Mount Gilead" (chapter 4, verse 1).

In this verse the king proves that God really did give him two scoops of wisdom. There's nothing smarter than complimenting your honeybunch's hair. In my experience, a husband can guarantee a warm and romantic marriage by remembering these two simple phrases:

"You're right, dear."

"Your hair looks great!"

A woman doesn't even require that you speak the same language if you can just write these two phrases on cards and hold them up at the appropriate time.

I don't know why complimenting a woman's hair is so important, except that maybe if you spent five hours a week working on something with curlers, a blow-dryer, and various chemical compounds, you'd want your soul mate to take notice.

However, I would have warned Sol not to go with the "flock of goats" idea. As I said before, when you draw comparisons with animals, you must use extreme care. During the eighties my wife had a haircut that made her look a little like a cocker spaniel. Do you think I was dumb enough to mention it? Well, not more than once, anyway.

"How beautiful your sandaled feet, O prince's daughter" (chapter 7, verse 1).

Once again, the king of romance shows us the way by taking notice of his sweetheart's new shoes. I don't know why that's important, but it is. This guy is a genius.

"Your waist is a mound of wheat encircled by lilies" (chapter 7, verse 2).

OK, I have to admit that I don't understand this line. Even *The SDA Bible Commentary* has to shrug its shoulders when it gets to this verse. But I think we can all agree that it's another compliment.

You look at the Song of Solomon, and you see compliments being thrown back and forth like wedding rice. While criticism chills a marriage, a few words of sincere appreciation can bring warmth and trust and intimacy. I guess you don't have to be the wisest man in the world to figure that out.

No Worries, Man

Have you ever noticed that even when men say they're worried, they don't sound worried? They make statements such as, "I believe we have reason for concern that the recession will deepen in the next business quarter." Doesn't exactly make your hair stand on end, does it?

Now, compare that with what a woman might say: "Why can't you remember to lock the back door at night? Don't be surprised if you wake up one morning and find that your family has had their throats cut by drug-crazed Nazi terrorists. Not to mention that *anyone* can walk in and swipe my spoon collection."

Women can bring an electrifying sense of national crisis to almost anything:

Wife: "Oh, no! We don't have a hostess gift for the Johnsons' dinner party. Do we want them to think we're uncivilized savages? We might as well show up wearing animal skins."

Husband: "What's a hostess gift?"

Wife, thinking: *I wonder if we could use this leftover hunk of Velveeta and make a convincing cheese log.*

Another example is women's concern over keeping their legs smooth and tan. This seems like excessive worrying to men, who will swagger around in shorts even when their legs make them look like Koko the gorilla.

Now, there may be some among you who disagree with the idea that women are more enthusiastic worriers than men. I may get a letter that says, "You have never seen my husband in the final minute of a tied football game. Often I have to calm him by rocking him in my arms and softly singing Doris Day songs."

OK, I see your point. But here is something you will definitely agree with: Whether you're a man or a woman, your worries will shrink to the size of that suspicious mole on your shoulder when compared to your worries when you become a parent. Suddenly you begin to think of ways— many of which defy the rules of physics—that a toddler could get his or her hand in the garbage disposal. You realize that almost everything in your house except the mattress is a choking hazard. And you hadn't noticed it before, but the neighbor's dog does look a *lot* like an Australian dingo.

Also, the great controversy between good and evil begins to focus more and more on germs. The other night at a restaurant, the father of an 8-month-old turned to his wife and asked, "Did you remember to wash the table with bleach?" If you bring a child with the sniffles to some churches, they'll mark a three-foot perimeter around the kid with biohazard tape.

In our own home we're a little worried about the future of our 2-year-old son because he refuses to obey authority figures. I've started a passbook savings account in case the day comes when I need to come up with bail money.

I know that the Lord made a point of telling us not to worry about what we're going to wear (women) and what we're going to eat (men). But He doesn't come right out and say, "Don't worry so much about your kids." One reason may be that He sympathizes with the worries of parents.

Not that He shares the same panicky, semirational fears that fill our heads, but He sympathizes in the sense that He is doing whatever He can to ensure the health and safety and salvation of His family.

There are parts of the Old Testament where you can see Him standing on the front porch yelling at the children of Israel, "Get back in the yard! If I told you once, I've told you a million times—don't play in the street. And Zedekiah, quit running with that sharp stick. You're going to put someone's eye out. [*Sigh.*] You kids are going to be the death of Me yet."

You Don't Say

My wife shocked me recently. She brought home a man to serve as an example of what a good husband should be like.

"Couldn't you just buy me a Gary Smalley book?" I asked. "It would be less humilating."

"Shhh," she replied. "He's talking to me."

"You're going shopping by yourself?" said Mr. Wonderful. "How about I tag along and carry your bags?"

When I heard him say that, I began to suspect that Mr. Wonderful was not human. Even Ghandi never volunteered to go shopping with the little woman. (Some say the whole idea of nonviolent resistance came to him while he was trying to avoid a trip to pick out new drapes.)

Mr. Wonderful, as it turns out, is a talking doll. Apparently, women buy him for the amusement of hearing a man say, "Here, you take the remote. As long as I'm with you, I don't care what we watch." Or "Actually, I'm not sure which way to go. I'll turn in here and ask directions."

Perhaps you're wondering, *Is there a Mrs. Wonderful?*

The answer is no. Mrs. Wonderful is not necessary, because men already have a special circuit in their brain that takes whatever a woman says and changes it to what they're hoping to hear. Scientists call this circuit the Reality Bypass Valve.

What the woman says: "We need a new four-wheel drive truck like we need a hole in the head. I thought we were going to pay off our credit cards."

What the man hears: "We need a new four-wheel drive truck. Why don't you pay for it with our credit card?"

What the woman says: "Dear, would you clean out the garage?"

What the man hears: "Dear, why don't you get some snacks and enjoy the ball game?"

What the woman says: "No."

What the man hears: "Yes."

Mr. Wonderful comes in a box that advertises, "He always knows just what to say."

There are some people like that. You find them on the morning shows telling an amusing anecdote about filming in the South of France, or explaining why a vote for them is a vote for more jobs, better schools and whiter teeth for all Americans.

Sometimes I imagine that I'm being interviewed on TV, and then I imagine the years of humiliation that would follow after I said the exact wrong thing. Such as the time I meant to ask a coworker if she had succeeded in having her car fixed, and instead asked if she had fixed her cat.

Opening my mouth is like letting a 2-year-old loose in a Mikasa store—there's a high risk of disaster. Sooner or later there will be misunderstandings, hurt feelings, or a restraining order. This is particularly distressing because I claim to be a Christian. And Christians are not supposed to be yelling into the phone, "Let me send you a dictionary because I think you've confused the meaning of 'customer service' with 'criminal neglect.'"

I've prayed for God to stop me from saying anything unkind. I'm not sure how that sort of prayer gets answered. Will I wake up one morning talking like Jimmy Carter? Or will God take the easy way out and just wire my jaw shut?

Perhaps you're also one of those people who lets words slip out of your mouth that you regret. Obviously, I don't have any advice. But I have found this clue in the book of Matthew. Jesus said: "Out of the overflow of the heart the mouth speaks."★

Apparently, if you want to speak like Mr. Wonderful, you need to have Him inside.

★ Matthew 12:34

To Hair Is Human

I recently took a few moments to reflect on my childhood and found that my memories generally consist of (1) opening Christmas presents, and (2) falling off my bicycle. If I were ever in danger and my life flashed before my eyes, the audio portion would sound something like this: "Thank you. Ouch! Thank you. Ouch! Thank you. Ouch!"

Of course, I have other childhood memories, one of which involves Dippity-Do—a product that proved that the hair-care industry had too much time on its hands. You might remember this gel (available in pink or blue) that you combed into your hair. After a few minutes this amazing, space-age polymer would harden your hairstyle into a shiny, bulletproof helmet. A person could go out into Hurricane Hugo, confident that even if their eyebrows blew off, the rest of their hair would remain as fixed in place as the Grand Tetons.

Dippity-Do made hair fascinating for a small boy. I remember sitting in third grade, taking rigid locks of hair in my fingers and snapping them like strands of dry pasta.

When Dippity-Do fell out of fashion, I lost interest in hair. To me, hair is like having a big fingernail on the top of your head that needs to be trimmed every once in a while.

I don't think I'm stepping out on a limb here when I say that men care less about their top fur than women. If you need proof, hunt down a school yearbook from the early seventies. Seen through the lens of time, it becomes obvious that the guys weren't even trying. While the girls spent hours ironing their hair to make it perfectly straight, the most effort you could expect from a guy was to trim his sideburns just before they reached his shoulders.

Here's a perfect example of the high standard women hold when it comes to hair. As my coworker Melynie was dressing for her wedding, her grandmother passed on this advice for a happy marriage: "Always get up an hour before your husband so that he never sees you without your hair fixed."

This counsel might be embraced by some women, but the only way a man is going to be motivated to get up an hour early to look after his hair is if it catches on fire.

I don't blame women for caring about hair. There's something almost noble in clinging to the hope that tomorrow will be a good-hair day. And this hope has captured the attention of modern industry and research.

Now that the Russians are no longer a threat, it appears that the scientists who once applied their energies to splitting the atom have now applied their brilliant minds to the problem of split ends. Having successfully put a man on the moon, we are now ready for the challenge of creating more body and shine.

For example, my wife has something called "Shaper Shampoo." On the back it states: "A cross-link between botanicals and babassu oil improves texture and builds high gloss."

On our bathroom vanity are aerosol bottles of "sculpting spray," something called "bodifying foam," a spray gel, and a "volumizing spray." Even if you have so few hairs on your head that you can count them as easily as your heavenly Father, these products promise to whip you up a mane like country music stars and My Little Ponies.

I'm pretty cynical about all that stuff. Which is what you would expect from a guy who gets his hair-care products from the Holiday Inn.

To me, life is like hair. We want to manage it, tame it, control it. We look to science and technology for help, but they often promise more than they can deliver. We read articles. We go to seminars that might have the one secret to success that we're missing.

But if we're ever going to get things straightened out, we need to turn the whole tangled mess over to a Higher Power. And I'm not talking about Dippity-Do.

Caller O.D.

We take too many things for granted. Right now, for example, you are taking the telephone for granted. (You are also taking elastic waistbands for granted, but they are not the subject of this article.)

The telephone is amazing. Think what it does to connect families! Even if your children are separated from you by mountains, rivers, and valleys, they can pick up the phone and seconds later be asking you for money.

Less amazing is the fact that even complete strangers can pick up the phone and ask you for money. I get calls that start out: "Hello, Mr. Pecan? I'm Officer So-and-so with the West Virginia State Troopers . . ."

I'm *this close* to blurting out, "Hey, I didn't know I was going 80! I was just following the traffic." Then he asks for money to help keep criminals off the streets. I'm thinking, *I've never been bothered by a criminal on the street. Can I donate to keep police off the phones*?

I also get lots of calls announcing that I'm eligible for a free cemetery plot. This is not the kind of call you want while you're waiting for the results of a treadmill stress test. Still, I say "yes" to all these offers. I'm hoping that one day I can put all the plots together and have enough room to park a mobile home. Resale might be a problem, but at least the deal includes free lawn care.

All I'm saying is that it's a risk to pick up the phone these days. What if it's a call from the church nominating committee putting you in charge of the youth department? Or it may be a call from your niece informing you that the check you sent for her graduation just bounced. Or it might be the poison control hotline asking for the exact ingredients of your potluck casserole.

But we take the risk and pick up the receiver because it *might* just be someone whose voice we want to hear. Like family. It might even be your father saying something like "Hi. How are you? Here's your mother." Fathers like to keep conversations concise because they can never forget when long distance was expensive.

You'll be saying, "Hello, Dad. We just called to wish you a happy birth—"

And he'll jump in, "Thanks for calling, but I don't want to run up your phone bill." *Click.*

It takes a child to see the telephone for the wonder that it is. Small children have an endless fascination with listening to the voices on the other end of the line. In fact, about all they do is listen because they haven't learned how to hold up their end of the conversation.

They usually pick up the phone with a simple "Hello?"

"Hello," you say in your friendliest voice. "Is this Ashley?"

"Yes." Long pause as Ashley waits to hear what else you will say.

"How are you today, Ashley?"

"Fine." Another long pause.

"What have you been doing?"

"Playing." A long pause. You hear the clock ticking on the mantelpiece. The shadows in the room move as the sun inches across the sky.

"Is there an adult there that I can talk to?"

"Yes."

"I'll give you a dollar if you'll go get them."

Many people have described prayer as a phone line to heaven. I see the similarities. Most of the time when God answers a call, it's somebody asking for something. And most of us don't stay on the line very long, as if we're afraid we're paying 30 cents a minute.

Of course, He's happy for every prayer. But perhaps He takes special pleasure in the ones that most resemble a child on the phone. Those times when we stop trying to keep up our end of the conversation, and we just hold the receiver, listening . . . listening for the voice on the other end.

Waiting for Mr. Write

I t is more blessed to give than to receive. While this is definitely true of homegrown zucchini, there are some things we would rather get than give. For example: Help with the dishes. A 30-minute massage. And mail.

I'm not referring to the kind of mail that offers you a new Visa card and a chance to spend yourself into indentured servitude. No, I'm talking about personal mail that begins by describing the weather or the grandkids or the amusing thing the dog did to the postal carrier.

The *only* reason that any of us bothers to check the mailbox is the hope that an honest-to-goodness personal letter will be inside. Nobody returns from the mailbox dancing with joy and singing, "Hurrah! The Alzheimer's organization remembered to send out their annual appeal. They must be feeling better."

Which brings me back to the fact that while everyone *wants* to get personal letters, the only people willing to write them are a handful of aunts from the Midwest. And I have a real fear that any moment now those aunts will discover five-cent Sundays and start using the phone like everybody else.

I'm hoping that day doesn't come soon because I like to get letters from Aunt Carolyn. She crams a lot more into an envelope than the post office had in mind when they set the price of a stamp.

When I opened the latest envelope from her, I found four snapshots of relatives—two of whom I'd never seen before—a card depicting a mouse in a dress, a list of funny things people said to her at work, a copy of a letter to someone else, a used-car ad, a cartoon, a newspaper clipping about the local weather, a page of Internet jokes, and an article from a 1942 *Better Homes and Gardens*.

"What next?" I wondered aloud. "A fragment from the Dead Sea Scrolls?" That's the kind of effort you put into staging a Christmas pageant for the whole church congregation, not into contacting one lousy nephew

33

who probably won't write back before the return of Halley's Comet.

Dispatching any kind of letter seems like too big a production to most of us. It takes time to compose a message. It takes energy to slap down that stamp.

That's why most of the letters we get each day come from people who are paid to write them. Right now I am looking at a letter that begins, "Dear Shredded Wheat 'N Bran Customer." It pretends to be signed by "The People of the Post Cereal Company" and expresses their great pride and satisfaction in being able to make a breakfast product with roughly the same fiber content as wicker furniture.

Here the letter gives up its personal nature and becomes mass media. Because that's where the money is.

So it seems almost heroic when someone decides to invest their time and energy in sending a message to an audience of one. Perhaps that's why we look forward to reaching into the mailbox and finding an envelope with our name scribbled on the front. We like that kind of personal attention.

President Harry Truman had the whole country to run, but he wrote a letter to his wife every day. And Jesus has the whole world to save, but He does it one person at a time.

Your Vacation
Questions Answered

The summer holidays are nearly upon us, so I will take this opportunity to answer your vacation questions. Not that anyone has actually asked me any vacation questions. But I wish they would. Nothing pumps up the male ego like getting a question.

Try this experiment: The next time you run into a male acquaintance, ask him why ice floats. The guy will preen like he just got invited to join the National Security Council and will follow you around for the rest of the day telling you everything he remembers from fifth-grade science class. You will probably have to fake a medical emergency to get him to change the subject.

Now, let's go to the vacation questions you might have asked if you had been considerate of my emotional needs:

Q. I would like to spend my holidays in a place where the people are warm and friendly. Where would you suggest?

A. You will find that everyone is friendly in Hawaii. Sociologists identify two reasons for the cheerful aloha spirit of the Hawaiian people. First, Hawaiians know that they always look better in swimwear than the tourists, who arrive on the beaches looking like they just popped out of a Pillsbury biscuit tube.

The second reason for their blissful attitude is that they are confident they will have all your money before you leave for home.

Q. Are you implying that the expenses of a Hawaiian vacation may break my budget?

A. Let me answer with another question. Are you perusing this magazine while a hairstylist prepares you for your next scene in a multimillion-dollar movie that is the latest installment in your wildly successful Hollywood career?

If you answered no, you can't afford Hawaii. But hey, don't let that stop you. Nobody who goes to Hawaii can afford it. Even I've been to Hawaii, though my wife and I owe our survival to the free snacks at time-share presentations.

Q. Can you suggest a family vacation spot?

A. In the old days, there were many places to take the family on vacation—the lake, amusement parks, and grandmother's house. Since then, all these destinations, including grandmother's house, have been moved to Orlando and are owned by the Walt Disney Company. In fact, you cannot even use the phrase "family vacation spot" without paying a royalty to Disney.

If you decide to visit the Magic Kingdom, remember that the entrance fee for a family of four requires that you present the deed to your home and grant Mickey Mouse power of attorney. In the future, Disney plans to simplify this awkward procedure by requiring all families with small children to pay them a second tithe. In return for 10 percent of their annual income, each family will receive a ration of park passes, an animated video based on pagan myth, and two stuffed Pooh characters.

Q. Wow. This sounds very expensive. Should I pass on vacation travel and just watch the Discovery Channel instead?

A. You *can* see exotic places on TV, but it's not the same as going there. It's the difference between reading a mission story and standing in the middle of a cannibal tribe yourself, trying to explain the advantages of a vegetarian diet.

I complain about the cost of vacation trips, but I can't pass them up. I relish the thought of firing up the old Honda and heading down the road to a promising destination.

We all need a promising destination. It was all right for Moses to spend time with the sheep. But how much better to be striking off across the desert with a pillar of fire above you and your eyes on the Promised Land!

Lest We Forget

Let us consider the brain. This wonderful organ can recall millions of items of information. Unfortunately, most of these items are advertising jingles. The stuff you really want to remember—such as where you parked the car at the airport—is gone with the wind.

That's been my experience, anyway. When it comes to memory, my mind has a mind of its own. I have come to it on bended knee saying, "Please, could you find someplace in those billions of neurons to store my telephone calling card number?"

It says, "Sorry, I just used the last of the space for a McDonald's jingle— 'Two all-beef patties, special sauce, lettuce, cheese, etc.'"

I say, "I don't need to know *that*. I'm a vegetarian!"

To paraphrase the apostle Paul, "Those things I want to remember, I do not."

For example, I wish I could remember people's names. Someone with a familiar face will approach me, and I'll desperately ring up to the brain. *What's the name of this person who is embracing me like a long-lost relative?*

I can almost hear the brain suppress a snicker as it says, "I'm not sure I have that file anymore. I think I had to clear it out to make room for your part in the church Easter play."

As further proof that our minds are as mischievous as a tentful of juniors, let me mention a little trick our minds pull on us called "Stop the music." This is where you start singing a song like "Born free, as free as the wind blows, as free as . . ." and suddenly you're humming because you have no idea what words come next. I think most people can sing only two songs clear through from memory: "Do, Lord" and the theme song to *The Beverly Hillbillies.*

Sometimes it seems as though a cheap computer hard drive would do a better job than the standard brain. You could instantly save important facts. Guys could remember the score of every football game. Women could remember every comment anyone made about their hair.

Another benefit is that it would take only a press of a button to delete the annoying little memories that brains cling to: for example, that embarrassing moment at your first academy banquet.

"But wait," I hear you saying. "What if you accidentally delete files you need?"

My answer to you is "Ha. That's the least of my worries because . . . ah . . . Could you repeat the question?"

What I mean is that my brain already deletes everything. It deletes birthdays, anniversaries, the reason I drove to the grocery store.

This is not so bad if you're a guy, because you can depend on your wife to remember for you. Solomon forgot to mention that a wife who is more precious than rubies is a wife who can tell you where you left your car keys.

Marriage is a good thing for the forgetful. My wife and I can sometimes remember an important fact if we combine our memories. "What's the name of that restaurant that so-and-so recommended?" I'll ask Lori. "I think it starts with an F." This is her clue that the name of the store will actually begin with any letter in the alphabet except F, and we work from there.

So, what can you do about a declining memory? Deep down, it worries me. What if this forgetfulness continues to creep over the whole mind until I can't even recognize the people I love? It happens.

But you know, even if I forget everything, God remembers. In fact, He remembers me so well that at His return, He will recreate me in every detail—a living, breathing, joyful citizen of the new earth.

Do, Lord, O do remember me.

Cover Your Eyes
While We Fast-forward

Many things in life seem like a good idea until you try them. Fat-free potato chips, for example.

It might also seem like a good idea to invite your church friends over on a long winter evening to enjoy a video. Let me share a few words of advice: DON'T EVEN THINK ABOUT IT! In my experience, the trip to Blockbuster never has a happy ending.

The first hint of trouble comes when you try to settle on a video everyone will watch. I mean, the last movie you could get Adventists to agree on was *The Sound of Music*, and some thought it was too soft on Catholics.

So choosing a movie becomes a delicate negotiation, with proposals and counterproposals that resemble a church board trying to decide on the carpet color for the new sanctuary.

"How 'bout this one?"

"I've seen it."

"How 'bout this one?"

"Nah, the colors on the cover seem garish."

These negotiations get particularly tough because men and woman have completely different tastes in movies. Women want bittersweet stories of love triumphing against impossible odds. Men want bittersweet stories of a man with a gun triumphing against impossible odds.

The women in the group will vote for a movie such as *Sarah, Plain and Tall*. "No thanks," the men will say. "Normally we love to watch movies about plain women who write letters about their cats, but tonight we'll just sit out in the car and listen to the ball game."

If you add children to the viewer mix, well, you suddenly realize how important it is for youngsters to have an early bedtime. Say about 6:00 p.m. Otherwise you're going to end up watching *Cars* one more time.

You might be tempted to skip the negotiations and just pick out a movie *you* want to watch. That's a bad idea because that leaves no one to share the blame when the movie ambushes you with a scene that makes everyone in the room cringe.

I'm always getting ambushed. About 30 minutes after I put the video in the player, the cold chill of embarrassment starts creeping up my spine. The actors are spouting language I haven't heard since the time I went Ingathering at a construction site. Or I am witnessing a murder in as much detail as possible without actually attaching a tiny camera to the bullet. Or the leading lady is participating with the leading man in an activity that, according to large parts of Leviticus and 1 Corinthians, they should not.

One time I gathered a houseful of friends—two of whom were local elders—in front of the TV, and the star actor arrived on the screen much like Eve makes her first appearance in *The Bible Story,* only without the chaste positioning of a rosebush.

There's nothing you can do to stop this. You can't get all the actors together beforehand and say, "Look, I'm having some respectable friends over, and I would appreciate it if everyone would keep their clothes on. And by the way—all of you with speaking parts—let me explain the third commandment."

In theory, the rating system should help me avoid embarrassment, but I can't figure it out. I suspect that the MPAA rating assigned to each movie involves someone's pet monkey and a box of Scrabble tiles.

Once I thought I had a clever plan to entertain without corrupting anyone's morals. I determined I would find an old movie—a classic from those innocent days when they didn't even need a rating system. The house was filled with friends when I presented a Cary Grant comedy that costarred two elderly and innocent-looking women. Well, it turned out that the dear women were poisoning men and burying them in the basement.

Why do movies so often ambush us with words and images that make us cringe? Perhaps it's because Hollywood doesn't have a lot in common with Christians. I'm afraid they think that a family value refers to the money you save when you buy the big box of Cheerios.

Once, when Paul was trying to straighten out the Corinthians, he asked them, "What does a believer have in common with an unbeliever?"

And sometimes when I watch a video with my Christian friends, I realize that we don't have much in common with Hollywood at all. And the sooner we push the "stop" button, the sooner we'll have a happy ending.

Note: My poor judgment in picking movies is evidenced by the fact that I have never seen *Chariots of Fire.*

A Guy's Guide to Computers

Nobody is begging for my advice, but I am a guy and therefore possess a deep instinctual need to "share" my opinion (even when people show subtle signs of disinterest, such as sticking their fingers in both ears and singing "The Battle Hymn of the Republic"). Today I would like to reach into my storehouse of wisdom and share some insight into the world of computers.

Where did the personal computer (PC) come from? Once upon a time computers were big expensive machines that performed excruciatingly dull jobs, such as printing insurance bills. Of course, big expensive machines elicit the same response in grown men that a stray puppy does in little girls—we want to bring it home.

When guys were finally able to buy their very own personal computer, they weren't exactly sure what to do with it. They considered sending insurance bills to their friends and then settled on the idea of using the computer as a typewriter. And so it remains to this day. My home computer is powerful enough to predict the earth's weather patterns. What do I use it for? To type.

Why do guys get so excited about computers? Good question. I just recently got a new computer at work, and I was so happy that you would have thought somebody had turned up my morphine drip. Carole, a coworker who's seen a lot of men get twitterpated by a new computer, puts the feeling in terms any woman can understand: "It's like when you find that perfect dress marked down from $400 to $69.99 . . . and it fits perfectly . . . and you already have shoes at home that match."

The only problem with this analogy is that the dress will remain in fashion for about three years. The computer will become obsolete a week from Tuesday.

Should I purchase a computer? What? Of course you should purchase a PC! This is particularly true if you have children. As any PC manufacturer can tell you, if your children don't learn to use computers, they'll be left behind in the march of civilization and be forced to gather roots and berries to survive.

What kind of computer should I buy? Computers, like children, are the most trouble when they are new. During the setup period they will lie on your desk squalling out beeps and error messages and failing utterly to do anything you want them to do.

So my solution is to adopt a computer that has already received the electronic equivalent of potty training. Go to the home of a friend who has coaxed all the software to work on their computer, and offer them $5,000 on the spot. You pay more money up front, but you save a bundle on Excedrin.

Can I learn how to use a PC without feeling foolish? The short answer is no. You can't help but feel silly when your 10-year-old nephew has already paid for his college education by trading stocks on the WorldWide Web, and you're staring at your monitor wondering why a talking paper clip is insisting on helping you type a letter.

How do I get on the Internet? You will find the most helpful information about getting on the Internet . . . um . . . on the Internet.

Are computers good or evil? Let me be quick to point out that computers are not the root of all evil. As anyone who listens to James Dobson knows, the root of all evil is a liberal Democrat.

But I'll tell you one thing: Computers are like big flower beds—they take all the time they can get.

And so the person who doesn't have a PC gets my grudging respect. By ignoring technology, they have more time for people. And that seems like a good thing.

You can take your fingers out of your ears now.

The New Olympic Games

The great thing about the Olympics is that they let men get caught up in a patriotic urge to conquer other nations without all the unpleasantness of actually going to war. In the old days, if a guy wanted to enjoy a surge of tribal pride, he had to find a sharp stick and go attack the village next door. It was a dirty, messy business that required a good medical plan and tended to take up all of one's weekend.

Now we modern men can let other people battle it out on the soccer field while we stay home, offering the occasional word of encouragement and advice from a La-Z-Boy. Unfortunately, this still eats up most of our weekends.

We guys love competition. And we don't care if the competition involves large, sweaty men wrestling each other or miniature teenage girls hurling themselves through the air like pizza dough. Men would watch a televised quilting bee if it had a competitive angle.

Women, on the other hand, aren't going to cancel a hair appointment every time there's a competition. I think that if the Olympic committee wants to catch the attention of more women, they're going to have to come up with more relevant games.

Let's take the discus throw as an example. Who cares how far a person can throw a boring piece of metal? Wouldn't it be far more entertaining to see how far contestants can throw a telemarketer?

What I'm suggesting is a shift to games that celebrate practical skills. For example, I don't know any women who play beach volleyball. But I know several who can make delicious jam. I admit that watching the Russian judge munching on toast and jam before giving a score wouldn't make good television. But I have a suggestion for that problem. During the jam-judging, the network can broadcast the women's shopping cart race.

The shopping cart race would resemble the 400-meter hurdle, only it would be more grueling. Mothers with two small children would begin at one end of a supermarket and get timed as they picked up items on a shopping list and maneuvered to the checkout. They would lose points every time a child broke into tears or sneaked an expensive box of breakfast cereal into the shopping cart.

Once again, relevance is the key. How many guys do you know who play water polo? But you probably know at least one man who feels he has a divine right to operate the television remote. So I'm suggesting an Olympic channel-chase competition.

Picture it. Several men sit comfortably in front of television sets that receive 200 channels. By rapid use of the remote buttons, they must try to follow the developments on more channels than their opponents. (Perhaps 200 channels would be too easy for most guys.)

Right now I can hear my critics saying, "Nobody will want to watch competitions like that. You'll never generate the passion that's poured into the current Olympic games."

How do you know? Maybe people said the same thing about mountain cycling and the balance beam. You see, you never know what will catch people's attention. Sometimes their passion is excited by things that are important—and sometimes by things that aren't.

Which may be one reason we humans need a God. God has a gentle way of leading us to those things that deserve our passion. He coaches us to win in matters of justice, mercy, and peace. And in many other matters, He shrugs His shoulders and lets us enjoy the game.

Note: How do athletes ever get to practice for the javelin throw? Don't their mothers come running out of the house shouting, "Quit throwing that pointy thing. You'll put someone's eye out"?

Easy Does It

An object at rest tends to stay at rest. This law of physics was discovered by Sir Isaac Newton while trying to get his teenager out of bed and off to school.

I sympathize with teenagers—I don't greet the morning with any great eagerness myself. The struggle to get up turns into kind of a hostage situation.

Brain: "Throw down the covers and come out with your eyelids up."

Body: "Ha! No one is going anywhere until you meet my demands."

Brain: "Be reasonable. It's time for work."

Body: "Here's my first demand: an alarm clock with a 40-minute snooze button."

Brain: "If you don't get moving soon, you'll be in for a career change that involves holding a cardboard sign at busy intersections."

Body: "You don't scare me! I'm staying with the Posturepedic."

I feel guilty about sleeping late, because my ancestors would be appalled by the very idea. They operated under the firm conviction that the best time to milk cows was 4:00 in the morning—an opinion that probably didn't receive any input from the cows.

Everybody from those early generations had a double dose of the work ethic. They often labored at two jobs and still showed up early for the church work bee.

Then my generation came along. We feel we've put in a full day if we vacuum the carpet. We're the reason they invented watermelons without seeds; we think it takes too much effort to spit them out. And our hearts are moved with sympathy for people who have to roll up their car windows manually.

It's as if each generation is reclining a little farther back in the La-Z-Boy of life. First you had the generation that baked a cake from scratch. Then came the generation that needed Betty Crocker to put the mix in a pretty box. Now we buy our layer cake already frosted in the freezer section and get annoyed that we have to wait for it to thaw.

If you think about it, we are probably the first generation that has the option of taking it easy. If our forefathers had decided to put off the harvest a couple days to relax on the golf course, they might have spent the winter gnawing on a boiled shoe.

Today few people are in danger of starving, and frankly, it takes the pressure off. I've noticed that even the greeters at Wal-Mart are loafing. The ones at my store look like they got tired of meeting new people about 10 minutes after opening time. They stare off in the direction of the snack bar, keeping their smiley stickers to themselves.

Yes, this is a great time to be lazy. We have shoes with Velcro instead of tie-up laces, and remote buttons that unlock the car so we don't have to deal with the tiresome nuisance of turning a key. Our only physical exertion is running around the family room looking for the TV remote.

These lazy times are possible because of our hard-working ancestors. We stand on the sweaty shoulders of those who cleared the land and built our roads. We benefit from the inventors and teachers and merchants who worked a little harder than they absolutely had to.

Sometimes love influences the choice between hard work and taking it easy. Whether it's Moses taking a whiny bunch of Israelites across the desert, or a mother rousting her kids out of bed and making them breakfast, an act of service has a way of rolling down through time, and maybe even across generations.

Dropkick Me, Jesus, Through the Goalposts of Life

Have you noticed that when parents drop a child on his head, they rarely mention it afterward? They never say, "Son, there was this time I put on too much hand lotion, and, well, you might have some problems when you start to take algebra."

Hey, I don't blame them. I do the same thing when I absentmindedly use my wife's toothbrush. Better to keep quiet about the whole matter and not stir up any unproductive concerns about gingivitis.

Anyway, I have a growing suspicion that my parents accidentally bounced me off the linoleum at an early age. I say this because there are several things that most people understand that leave me confused. These include: (1) Why would anyone *want* to eat a shrimp? and (2) Why is professional football important?

If a husky man wants to roughhouse with other husky men on a large lawn . . . well, fine. But I'm not going to clear my schedule on New Year's Day to watch them do it. I just don't *get* football.

So naturally, I won a trip to the Super Bowl.

To be absolutely accurate, the trip was won by my wife—who wouldn't know the difference between a field goal and field corn. She simply took me along to increase the level of irony. It was like two vegetarians inheriting a chain of steak houses.

Well, on the Sunday before the big event, Lori decided to do a little research by tuning in the play-off games on TV.

At the moment she began watching, she was the same wife I had always known—a polite, poetic creature who never had a competitive moment in her life (except for the time at a yard sale when another woman wanted to buy the same piece of Tupperware). Then, as the games continued, she started cheering and shouting at the TV screen in an entirely new language. Football phrases such as "blitz," "interception," and "permanent knee injury" began to come out of her mouth.

I even caught a little of the spirit. So we were both feeling pretty enthusiastic when our plane touched down in the Super Bowl city. And we met people who were even more enthusiastic than we were—people who wore watermelons on their heads and painted their faces in colors that are normally reserved for Mexican handcrafts.

It was a good football game . . . as far as we could tell. Our seats were so far above the field that we actually had to get permission from air traffic control to move in and out of our row.

We enjoyed a stirring halftime show sponsored by Walt Disney World. Thousands of paper doves fluttered down through the air, emphasizing the theme of global peace and harmony, after which time both teams ran back on the field and began knocking each other down.

The score was close in the final minutes of the game. The cheering got so loud that it was like sticking your head in a giant leaf blower. And strangely enough, part of the cheering came from us—two people who didn't know they were fans.

That whole Super Bowl experience was a thrill that fell into our hands even though we didn't pursue or deserve it.

The Bible says to seek and we shall find.

But what's so wonderful about grace is that it helps us find the joys that we don't have the sense to seek. It opens the right doors when we are busy knocking somewhere else. It helps us score when we don't even know how to play the game.

Live Dangerously—
Sleep on a Mattress

According to the statistic that I just made up, 38 percent of women feel that their lives are boring. Well, no wonder. We live in an age when there are simply not enough things that can eat you.

In the old days, when Mrs. Daniel Boone left the house, she had a good chance of meeting a bear. That made her life much more exciting than yours or mine. Even a church finance committee can be thrilling if you're anxious about making it home afterward without wringing bear saliva out of your shirt.

But today in North America there's nothing that will eat you. You can travel far and wide, and never be in danger from any of God's creatures—unless you count the bacteria in those interstate restrooms.

So we're living in a country that's as safe as a parked Volvo, and frankly, we will perish from boredom if we don't discover some element of danger in our lives. That's why we can be grateful for the Internet.

Take the example of my friend Larissa. She had a fairly ho-hum existence until she came across an Internet site that exposed the dangers of her office computer. According to the Web site, computer monitors send off some kind of death ray that will turn your eyes into Hostess Sno Balls. Suddenly going to work has an exciting sense of peril for Larissa, and her donations to National Camps for the Blind have increased dramatically.

I recently came across a Web site that added a bracing sense of danger to my holiday celebrations. This site alerted me to the hazards of spruce Christmas trees. Apparently, spruce needles are so sharp that if a child should accidentally brush against the tree—mothers, you may want to avert your eyes to avoid the horror I am about to describe—the child will experience a painful, pricking sensation on exposed areas of his skin!

Of course, the Internet story that has created the greatest thrill for us all is the e-mail about the missing kidneys. I'm referring to the story about the guy who, after a night on the town, wakes up in a tub of ice with scars on his back and a note around his neck saying that his kidneys have been stolen.

I am somewhat suspicious about this story, because the kidney thieves seem very considerate. First, they stitch up the wounds; then they leave a helpful note suggesting the victim call 911. I'm surprised they didn't leave a prescription for antibiotics and an appointment card for a post-op visit.

Perhaps you've also noticed that television news shows try to whip up a sense of danger in everyday life. I tuned in the other night to hear this teaser: "Are you sleeping on something dangerous? Your bed could turn into a ball of fire!" The local Fox station thought it would be amusing to run this story on the 10 o'clock news, just before their viewers tucked themselves in for the night.

Well, I had to watch. A very serious investigative reporter demonstrated how your mattress and bed linen will catch fire if—surprise—you leave an open flame underneath the bed. So there you have it: another reason not to invite the Pathfinders to have their wienie roast in your bedroom.

On this earth we're pretty safe, but never perfectly safe. There is always enough danger to give us a thrill of fear and a rush of anxiety—which may be why Jesus put a few lines in his Sermon on the Mount about not being anxious about tomorrow. He seemed to know that even in a time when lions or bears aren't roaming the streets, people can still get eaten alive by worry.

Improve Your Memory,
If Not Your Hair

I have 100 billion brain cells. My question is: "What do they do with their time?" They certainly aren't remembering where I left my cell phone.

Generally, our memory is as reliable as that of a 2-year-old flower girl. And I think I know why—memory is not the brain's real job. Memorizing is strictly a volunteer effort for brain cells. Their real employment probably centers on avoiding blame.

Say you back the car into the garage door. Immediately all the brain cells swing into action to find a way to blame your shoes, the car, or the Bush administration.

Whenever a memory function is required, the brain is forced to round up volunteer neurons. It may call a neuron asking if it would please remember the password for your eBay account. The neuron explains that it would like to say yes, it really would, but right now it's avoiding blame for a kitchen fire.

So the brain says, "That's fine. Have a good evening." It then proceeds to call the next neuron. This neuron would also like to help, but claims it has been on disability since a big slice of chocolate cheesecake.

After polling all 100 billion of its cells, the brain finds just enough volunteers to remember that your password is the name of a grandchild, but not enough to remember *which* grandchild.

Fortunately, there are ways you can improve your memory.

1. Stop shampooing your hair. According to an NBC news reporter (who probably isn't motivated to exaggerate a story in order to get in front of a national audience and achieve fame), an ingredient in shampoo called DEA might soak into your head and inhibit the growth of memory cells.

This makes perfect sense to me. I've been shampooing every day for years, and I'm to the point now where I make my wife and child wear name tags.

2. Use mnemonic devices. These are named in honor of Mnemosyne, the Greek goddess of spelling bees. One mnemonic device is "Righty, tighty; lefty, loosey," which helps me keep things straight when conversing about politics.

Another example is the "image-name" device, which is helpful when you meet new people. Let's say you are introduced to Mrs. Swartugick at a potluck. While you enclose her hand in a firm handshake, you create a mental image to help you remember the name. For example, you picture a giant lollipop shaped like Norman Rockwell's left ear. This gives you SWeet and ART. Now for the next part of the name: TUG. Well, that's easy because right now the woman is tugging her hand out of your firm handshake. "Wait," you say. "Where are you going? There's no need to be frightened. I'm just working on an image for 'ICK.'"

3. Do something embarrassing. Vicki tells the story about going out to eat with the executive staff at her new job. A few minutes after everyone had been seated in the Mexican restaurant, the waiter appeared with chips and dips. *This is nice,* thought Vicki. *Free chips before the meal.* She took a handful and politely passed the dish around the table. She thought she was making a good impression until her boss leaned over and whispered, "Do you realize that's my entrée you're offering everyone?"

Shame is the very best way to sear something into your memory. No matter how often Vicki shampoos, she will never forget this incident.

I think shame is also the reason many saints never quite forget their sins. On the other hand, the wicked, like the Fox television network, have always been known as those who have no shame. So they're prone to forget. Why does God let them off so easy?

The doctrine of the judgment helps make sense of this. The judgment is God's memory device for those who have gone through life passing blame instead of admitting shame.

And for those who have remembered and repented from their sins all along, it is the time when God says, "Sins? What sins? They seem to have slipped my mind."

The Man Who Knew Too Much

I know too much for my own good. This includes my newfound knowledge of haloacetic acid, which, according to the Environmental Protection Agency, has caused many laboratory animals to earn the nickname Lumpy.

The subject came up when my water department thought they should mention that our drinking water had *four times* the maximum level of the contaminant allowed by law. Of course, that was last April, they pointed out, and the situation has improved since then. "Please don't worry about a thing," they said, "and accept with our compliments a free refrigerator magnet with the seven warning signs of cancer."

I appreciate the water department's openness, but I wish they had kept their information to themselves. It's a tragedy. It's in the past. Let's just forget about it. I feel the same way about my high school haircut.

I also get too much information from the Internet. One Web site says that dentists recommend that you keep your toothbrush at least six feet from the toilet because of the spray caused by flushing. Well, immediately I had to go get a tape measure. My worst fears were confirmed. For the past 10 years my toothbrush has been five inches too close to the toilet.

If only the sweet veil of ignorance had kept this information from me. For one thing, I wouldn't have had to gargle through an entire bottle of Listerine. And for another, I wouldn't feel compelled to keep my toothbrush in a Tupperware container in the attic.

On second thought, what kind of toilet throws spray *six feet*? Are we talking about the porcelain equivalent of Old Faithful? If these dentists have really seen such a fixture, they should put some colored lights under that thing and charge admission.

Perhaps I should return to my point, which is—let me check my notes—oh, yes, that sometimes we get too much information. I refer you to the case of Mr. Jordheim, a music teacher who spent several weeks in China. One morning he was making pleasant conversation with his host when he mentioned that he had particularly enjoyed the hash browns at breakfast.

"Ah," replied the host, who then moved on to other subjects.

A couple days later Mr. Jordheim felt compelled to speak again of those wonderful hash browns. This was too great a temptation for his host, who then revealed that, no, those were not hashbrowns. Those were shredded intestines.

This is one case in which the mysteries of the Orient would have been best kept that way.

The truth is that there are many pieces of information that we are happy to do without. We don't want to know how much we *could* have saved with coupons. We don't want to know how many people were offered the job before us. And we don't really want to know all the shades of meaning in our teenage daughter's poetry.

To take it one step further, there are things we know about ourselves that we'd just as soon forget. Such as that time in the eighties when we actually used the phrase "gag me with a spoon" in polite conversation.

And let's not even talk about our sins—those spiteful words and shameful deeds that our conscience keeps on file. Of course, there are ways to cope with guilt. One is to ignore it until it goes away. The other is to "draw near to God with a sincere heart in full assurance of faith, having our hearts sprinkled to cleanse us from a guilty conscience."* When you know too much about yourself, there is nothing more comforting than to know forgiveness.

---

* Hebrews 10:22

Did You Say Something?

Have you ever been lending an ear to a friend—nodding your head with interest and maintaining sincere eye contact—and realized that you were, in fact, not listening? It's as if your brain takes a 20-second vacation to the Bahamas and makes it back to the office just in time to hear the other person say ". . . so be sure to avoid eating any of that until they trace the killer bacteria."

This happens to me quite often. It even happens while I am listening to my wife—which, let me tell you, does nothing to enhance the sweet bonds of marriage.

Maybe it's a side effect of age, like rheumatism and an affection for Cracker Barrel restaurants. Or maybe it's because there's a lot of talking in the world, and it's hard to take it all in.

For instance, consider those automated phone-answering systems. The voice might be the most pleasant in the world, but the subject matter lacks drama. So after the first 60 seconds of hearing which buttons to push, my mind has run off to join the circus.

And what about those safety instructions they give you on airplanes, describing which end of the metal buckle should be firmly grasped? If you can listen all the way through that spiel with rapt attention, your Ritalin dosage is too high.

Sermons provide another way to test a person's attentiveness. I take great pleasure in reminding my friend Larry about the time I saw him doze off during a sermon on the subject of—get this—the evils of sloth.

I think God in His mercy protects pastors from knowing how far the minds of the congregation wander during sermons. While the pastor is preaching sanctification, people in the pews might be pondering subjects of less eternal significance, such as *Who's supposed to be sharpening the pencils by the offering envelopes?*

I know it would put a lot of pressure on clergy, but what if we could measure the attentiveness of the congregation in the same way that TV programs measure their audience? At the end of the service, the pastor would get a report of the percentage of people who tuned in: sermon—71 percent; children's story—84 percent; potluck announcement—99 percent.

If I may say so, the whole problem with lecturing is that it's so one-sided. In any other verbal encounter that lasts for more than five minutes, most of us expect an opportunity to mention our back pain and the accomplishments of at least two or three grandchildren. If there's going to be talking, we like to take turns.

Person 1: "I've got a bit of a headache."

Person 2: "Yeah, well, I've got this mole that looks a little like the state of Kentucky."

Person 1: "Oh, really? Well, in the summer of '87, I canned about 20 quarts of peaches."

Person 2: "That reminds me—do you know that little Buster can play 'Cherokee Nation' on the piano?"

Person 1: "Great. Say, does this sweater make me look fat?"

Apparently, even if you have give and take in a conversation, it doesn't mean anyone is listening. And listening is a good thing. We all know that. We expect God to listen to our prayers all the time, and we take for granted that His attention doesn't wander.

But we will have a richer relationship with Him if we add Bible study to our prayer life. In that way we're listening to what God has to say—even if our attention does wander from time to time.

My Photographic Memory

What would you save if your house caught fire? I think that men and women would answer that question differently. Maybe men would be quicker to save practical things such as the bank papers, whereas women would be more concerned about items with sentimental value—such as the children.

My wife has already told me to save our photographs. Unfortunately, we have so many albums that it's going to take me several trips out of the house. And I know I'll end up trying to convince the firefighters that I *must* go back into the burning building one more time to rescue a framed picture of my mother-in-law.

We take a lot of photos. This is what we do in place of having a functioning memory. Let's say that we're having a wonderful vacation at the beach. I know that my brain will take the memories from the vacation and file them in the same place as the lyrics to "The Star-Spangled Banner," thereby ensuring that I'll never recall them again. But if I take pictures, my wife and I can look at them years later and say, "When were we at the beach? And who's that person with their arm around us?"

Now, if you're really serious about remembering the sun-dappled joys of each passing day, get a video camera. I've been busy documenting my life for several years and, as of today, have accumulated 68 hours of home video. It consists mostly of people opening Christmas presents and a fascinating tour of the sidewalks of Disney World when I forgot to switch off the camcorder.

I guess Lori and I have some kind of vague notion that when we move into a nursing home, we'll want to get out the videos and fondly remember the past. But when the time comes, I think we'll prefer to watch *Matlock* with the rest of the residents.

Television is more interesting than home videos for many reasons, not the least of which is that TV people get professional help with their hair. So it's hard to find any ambulatory person who will sit still for a home video. Force your friends to watch 40 minutes of shaky footage from your visit to The Museum of Amish Cooking Utensils, and the next thing you know, they've all got caller ID and the relationship is over. Of course, if you have a video that shows you getting smacked in the head with a golf ball, that's a different story.

Perhaps a better way to share your memories is to take your photos and iron them onto T-shirts. Wear a new one to the office each day, and by November your workmates will have seen all the highlights of your Caribbean cruise.

It's hard to comprehend that not so very long ago people didn't have photographs. If your mother said you were a pretty baby, nobody could produce evidence that you really looked like Bob Newhart. Also, your children could never make fun of the clothes you wore in high school.

On the other hand, you couldn't see how happy you were as a child playing on the merry-go-round, or how beautiful your grandmother looked at her wedding. There are reasons to capture these moments that pass by so quickly. No wonder we would want to save them from a burning building.

If we feel that way about pictures of people, imagine how God feels about the people themselves. Right now, His Spirit is working to draw each of us into His kingdom. If you think He's going to wait for a fire to save us, you would be wrong.

If It Weren't for Potluck, I'd Have No Luck at All

When I imagine the heavenly banquet table, I see lots of Corningware and smell Special K loaf. I guess I have a close association in my mind between gatherings of the saints and potlucks. And if we do get together for potlucks in the new earth, then you can be sure someone will show up with a casserole.

Casseroles are the culinary melting pot of the church. No matter what lies lurking in your cupboard or refrigerator at this moment, someone has made a casserole out of it. Tater Tots, Nuteena, leftover spaghetti, zucchini abandoned on your front porch by neighbors, Hi Ho crackers, breakfast cereal—anything seems to work if you add a can of cream of mushroom soup.

I myself use this grayish goop in my sauerkraut casserole, a dish that I have stopped bringing to potluck because the smell makes people's eyes water. I began to think it might be too strong for the average taste when I noticed that it burned holes through the aluminum foil covering the dish. (I'm not kidding.)

Nobody wants to bring an unpopular dish to a potluck. Only poetry can capture the despair of a cook who must carry home a casserole dish with only a corner eaten out of it. To quote my aunt Alvaine, "It's like a slap in the face."

On the other hand, nothing matches the thrill of seeing that your casserole dish stands empty at the end of a potluck. It's as if the whole world stands up and shouts, "We love your cooking!" Suddenly, the skies seem bluer and the birds sing louder and you forget the inferiority complex you've had since the sixth grade.

Naturally, cooks strive to achieve potluck popularity. For example, Aunt Alvaine has learned that her dishes go faster at a potluck if she adds two sticks of real butter to the recipe.

Another surefire way to make your dish more popular is to add cheese. Now, I realize that cheese excites controversy among the health-conscious. Some will not let the substance pass their lips, earning the respect of cardiologists everywhere. But most people I know are not so strict. They will shove aside the weak and infirm to get the last serving of a really cheesy lasagna.

Yes, cheese has mighty powers of attraction. I believe that you can bring *anything* in a casserole dish—grass clippings, fiberglass insulation, whale meat—and if you cover it with enough cheese, people will shovel it on to their paper plates.

Last week I went to a potluck that had 98 dishes (not including those on the dessert table), and the first one scraped clean was a container of Kraft macaroni and cheese—which proves that a food item only has to be the *color* of cheese to achieve popularity.

While everyone wants their dish to be well received, I've never noticed open competition between cooks. I think this is because women preside over potlucks. Things would change if men did the cooking.

If the more competitive sex took over, you would see us skipping the sanctuary service to prepare exotic creations over a hot stove. I can imagine the lights dimming in the fellowship hall toward the end of potluck as Elder Smith makes a dramatic entry with flames shooting up from his Cherries Jubilee. Later, you hear a round of applause as Deacon Johnson brings out a Baked Alaska on a sterling silver platter. And men wouldn't give away recipes. You'd see some wheeling and dealing: "I can't let my rice pilaf recipe go that cheap, but if you throw in that old boat motor . . ."

I've seen some potlucks organized with military efficiency. Everyone whose last name begins with A to C is instructed to bring a yellow vegetable, those with names D, E, and F must bring a salad made with lime Jell-O, and so on.

But at most potluck affairs, participants are left to bring what the spirit dictates. Usually, things work out fine.

I think you can say the same about the church body. Some of us are far from perfect (our characters are a little cheesy, so to speak). Others wonder if they have any spiritual gifts to contribute at all. And still others feel that what they *do* have is not appreciated. But when the Master of the heavenly banquet table brings us together in service, we find that we have everything we need, and we need everything we have. It's like a potluck, only different. Luck has nothing to do with it.

A Guy's Guide
to the Temperaments

I magine that your church organizes a series of weekend seminars. Which would you attend?

A. The Joys of Preparing Your Will

B. Creating Colorful Desserts With Barley Green

C. Discover Your Personality Type!

If you answered "C," you are not alone. Of the many subjects being presented in church seminars, none has more popular appeal than this business about being sanguine, choleric, etc. I think it taps into the human tendency to be fascinated by every little detail about ourselves—except for our IQ, which some of us would just as soon not know.

I want to say right off that I'm a big believer in the temperaments. I'm a believer because people have exactly the attitude toward their temperaments that you would expect.

The sanguine chirps, "Hey, I'm a sanguine! Isn't that funny!"

Melancholy people bemoan their temperament in the same disappointed tone that they use to complain about losing the Publisher's Clearing House Sweepstakes for another year in a row.

Pick up the phone to call a choleric, and she'll declare, "Yes, I'm a choleric. Say, while I've got you on the phone, would you be potluck host next month?"

And when you try to ask a phlegmatic about his temperament, he shrugs, "I don't know. You decide."

Men don't seem to explore the temperaments with the same enthusiasm as women do. I put this down to the male distaste for introspection. We generally have very little interest in what is going on inside us unless we have the stomach flu.

I know more about the temperaments than most men because relatives send me Florence Littauer tapes. The tapes have been recopied so many times that it's hard to tell whether she's speaking English or Hungarian, but I get the general idea. I suspect that if Mrs. Littauer knew how many tapes have been copied without paying her royalties, she would no longer be a sanguine.

I have even taken tests to determine my temperament. Once it took me 30 minutes to answer all the questions. I'm concerned that these tests are so long and complicated that they distract men from more important duties, such as deciding which NASCAR number to put in the back window of their pickups. So I have devised a simple temperament test that you can give a man in 15 seconds. Here it is:

1. Do you have no interest in taking this test? (You are a phlegmatic.)

2. Are you too busy to take this test? (You are a choleric.)

3. Are you already bored by this test and thinking about what flavor of Doritos you want at your Super Bowl party? (You are a sanguine.)

4. Have you decided to pay no attention to this test because it is imprecise? (You are a melancholy.)

Once men know about temperaments, I think it makes us more forgiving of quirks displayed by the women in our lives. For instance, if my wife forgets to pick me up at the airport for two days, I'm slightly more likely to shrug it off and say, "Well, she's a sanguine. She can't help it."

We might even be able to cheerfully endure someone like my choleric aunt Rose, who has perfected the art of driving a car without the inconvenience of actually operating the controls. "Slow down," she says repeatedly to the driver until he brings the car to a complete stop. Then she taps him on the shoulder and says, "Hurry up. We don't want to be late."

This temperament thing also reminds me that we need all kinds in our families and in our churches. We wouldn't want to be surrounded by people just like us. I have nightmares about going on vacation with a bunch of phlegmatics like myself, and we spend the whole time saying: "What do you want to do today?" "Oh, I don't care. What do *you* want to do?"

God uses variety to great effect. It reminds me of a well-decorated home. A melancholy person takes different pieces of furniture and accessories and combines them in a way that—by comparison—makes my home look like the waiting room at a muffler shop. In a similar way, God creates all varieties of people—melancholy, sanguine, short, tall, red, yellow, black, and white. Then He puts them together to make His kingdom. It's going to be beautiful.

Moses Goes Back to Church

If you're thinking about returning to church, you have to ask yourself, "Do I really want to go back and deal with all the hypocrites, Pharisees, and vegetarians?" Of course, you can find the same kinds of people at a Greenpeace rally; but still, you should think it over.

Consider the experience of Moses, who was raised in the Hebrew "church." Eventually he left home and landed a high position in government. You would think the church members would be happy for him, but every time he came around the old neighborhood, it was always the same. Someone would make a comment about his "worldly" Egyptian haircut, or the fact that he wore too much jewelry, or that his linen skirt was too short.

He tried to explain that *everybody* at the palace wore these kinds of clothes, but the saints just said, "If all your friends were jumping off the Great Pyramid of Giza, would you do it too?"

He probably felt like saying, "I'd rather jump off a pyramid than build one." But thankfully, his mother had raised him to be polite, so he kept his mouth shut.

The one thing that finally pushed him over the edge, though, was the gossip. He couldn't go to a party barge down on the Nile or get in a fight with an Egyptian taskmaster without the news traveling all over the church. One night he packed up and left town. Which, of course, made the rumors even worse.

* * *

If our narrative ended here, it would resemble many stories about individuals leaving the church. A common element in these tales is a congregation that wears on our hero's nerves like an MCI telemarketing campaign.

It would be nice if all church members were positive and fun-loving people who accept you for who you are. But finding people like that isn't easy, and when you do, they expect a large tip at the end of the cruise.

Real people are annoying. And I'm not just talking about street mimes and Osama Bin Laden. Every human has an annoying side. They might clear their throat too often, or they might program their cell phone to play Barry Manilow tunes. They might feel compelled to tell you that a dermatologist can "get rid of that mole in a jiffy."

Even people to whom you have pledged eternal love can get on your nerves if you try to wallpaper a bathroom with them.

Often the problem starts with words. Such as the time in a Midwestern town when one of the saints approached a long-haired deacon to say, "A person who looks like you shouldn't be allowed to take up the offering."

"Fine," said the young man. He handed the older member his collection plate and walked out the door. Thirty-five years passed before he was seen back inside that church.

"How can anybody say something so rude?" you ask. There are some people who mean no harm—and I include myself in this group—but who let their mouth run like a country dog. In my case it seems that my brain says to my mouth, "You go on ahead. I'll catch up with you later."

That's the best explanation I can give for the time I told my wife that her new perm made her look like a cocker spaniel. Eventually, she let me back into the apartment, and I'm grateful. I will say only one thing in my defense: It was the eighties, and more people should have been speaking out against the prevailing hairstyles.

Whenever the mouth runs off without adult supervision, it often says something judgmental. A good example is the following statement: "I saw you brought lasagna to potluck. The Spirit of Prophecy says that people who eat ricotta cheese will not see the Second Coming."*

Being judgmental is an almost unstoppable natural impulse, much like the need to talk about grandchildren. I sometimes judge six or seven people before noon—more if I hear any news about Congress.

I mention all this to say that participating in a church family is like walking through Berkeley in a mink coat. Sooner or later, someone is going to say something judgmental.

* * *

Moses spent 40 years herding sheep before God promoted him to herding people. As is common in church work, the promotion did not come with a raise.

The poor guy had been back with the Israelites for only a couple weeks before they started judging him again. He had been trying to negotiate the release of his people, and Pharaoh started making things tough around the workplace.

The Hebrews came to Moses and said, "May the Lord look upon you and judge you! Pharaoh is going to kill us, and it's all your fault."

Moses could have thrown up his hands and gone back to his old job. At least the sheep didn't blame him for everything. He was just trying to help.

Instead, he sympathized with the Hebrews and called on God to fix the situation. Soon the whole tribe was marching through the Red Sea.

Six weeks later the people were complaining again. "If we were only back in Egypt," they wailed.

"But you were slaves, remember?" said Moses. "You carried bricks all day."

"Yeah, the work was hard," they replied, "but the company cafeteria was great!"

The Hebrews continued with their critical and generally annoying behavior for 40 years, and Moses stuck with them the whole time.

In fact, when God was considering wiping the slate clean and starting over with a less annoying group of people—"Those Babylonians seem really nice," He might have said—Moses stuck up for the Israelites. "Please forgive their sin," he pleaded. "But if not, then blot me out of the book you have written."

Why was Moses willing to give up his life for this bunch of whiners?

I imagine that part of it had to do with the burning bush. Tim Lale, coauthor of *Ten Who Left*, makes this observation about the people he interviewed: "All of those who eventually returned to church fellowship had an experience of awakening with God."

Each of them came to a place in the desert where they could sense the heat and smell the smoke of their own burning bush. Their relationship with God was revitalized; *then* they rejoined a community of believers.

Danny Palakiko had that kind of experience. He was a teenager when he gave up on the Adventist Church. The thing that really annoyed him was that he wasn't supposed to eat pork. His friends on the island of Maui made some really good pork. And he liked the octopus, too.

Palakiko skipped around other religions for a decade or more. Then he came back to visit his old congregation. "When I walked in the door of the church, the presence of the Holy Spirit was so imminent—so easily discerned," he remembers. He had to stay.

Wasn't he still annoyed by the other members? Didn't he disagree with some of their ideas? Danny has an answer for that: "You get to a point where you realize that you're missing something that you need. So you're willing to put all that other stuff aside."

* * *

I hope all your seat belts are securely tightened, because I'm going to shoot off in another direction. Strangely enough, all this reminds me of marriage. On my wedding day, my father-in-law announced that when I married Lori, I married the whole family. This took me by surprise, as I had purchased only two tickets for the honeymoon.

But he was right. I do spend a lot of time with Lori's family. Luckily, they're nice folk, and we get along just great (as long as we all don't try to pick up a restaurant check at the same time).

But it really doesn't matter whether they are nice or not. I would have married my wife even if her family were a tribe of murderous, head-hunting cannibals. It's the relationship with *her* that's important. And if that means we have to hike into the mountains of Borneo for Christmas, well, so be it.

Anyway, are you thinking about going back to church? Well, don't go back because you think we've become a fun bunch of handsome, fashionable, and witty people since you've seen us last. We can still be annoying and judgmental. Sometimes we're about as much fun as reading volume nine of the *Testimonies* on a Saturday night. Sure, we want to worship with you again, but there's a good chance we'll fall short of your ideals.

There's only one reason to come back, and that is to be closer to the Bridegroom. The rest of us are just the in-laws.

---

* It's hard to improve on author Anne Lamott's response to people who make judgmental statements: "Hey, you know the difference between you and God? God never thinks He's you."

"Pray for Me,
Miss Moneypenny"

I'm beginning to doubt that James Bond is a real person.

Here's the thing that tipped me off: He never prays. A guy his age should be praying that his coworkers don't find out that he uses Grecian Formula. And wouldn't those times when the villain dangles him over a pool of hungry sharks result in fervent supplications to the Almighty? Then again, maybe he *is* praying, only it's one of those stealth prayers like the one you say before digging into lunch at the Hard Rock Café.

I'm just pointing out that there is a suspicious lack of religion in Mr. Bond's life. If a normal person escaped certain death at the hands of Dr. Evil for the fourteenth time, he would begin to think that God has a plan for his life. He would probably give up the spying business and enter the ministry—maybe write a book and speak at weekend retreats. "Every day I was saving the world from destruction," he would say during his presentation, "but I still wasn't happy. After the supermodels left my hotel suite, I would sit alone and cry."

His story—especially the part before his conversion—would hold the attention of the men. James Bond plays to our fantasies—fast cars, blowing things up, and, of course, attractive women to assist us in these endeavors. Throw in an all-you-can-eat buffet, and it would be perfect.

He can do it—*alone*

But there is another part of the fantasy that is irresistible—it's the idea that James is suave and debonair enough to handle any situation on his own. To help you understand why this concept is so seductive, let me just say that James Bond is a man who never has to stop at a gas station and ask for directions.

That is our manly ideal. In reality, we can't even handle crabgrass without professional help. I remember one time when I took it upon myself to defrost the refrigerator. Like James Bond, I was confident of my ability to deal with the situation. I started the job by using my wife's hair dryer. After 10 minutes and two tablespoons of melted water, I decided to get serious. I brought out a chisel and a hammer. Soon I was throwing out big chunks of frost. Unfortunately, I also had to throw out the refrigerator. In my suave and debonair way, I had pounded the chisel through one of the Freon lines.

We must deal as best we can with the gap between heroic abilities (Mr. Bond can disarm a nuclear weapon while holding his breath underwater) and our own lack of ability ("H'mmm, how am I supposed to open this e-mail attachment?"). Sometimes we just lie to ourselves and believe that we can handle the situation. And at other times—when our frailty is inescapable—we pray.

I teach youth in church, and these teens will pray about everything. Last week someone's hair was recommended as a subject for intercessory prayer. Then there was the very confident varsity athlete who would pray that the opposing team wouldn't get their feelings hurt when they lost the upcoming game. Of course, there are prayers about math tests, the weather, and sick grandparents.

Every day, we decide what aspects of our life we will handle by ourselves, and which will become a matter of prayer. Some of us believe that the sooner we come before the throne of grace and ask for directions, the better. And for the rest of you who think you can manage your life without divine help, all I can say is "Are you for real?"

A Little Something
for the Pain

L et's talk about suffering. People are mostly against it. Still, they may find that suffering is forced upon them by war, famine, or an ambitious exercise program. Some individuals—and here I'm referring to people who are experiencing natural childbirth—wonder how God can be a God of love and still allow suffering in the world.

Actually, lots of people ask this question. "There are patients hurting in the hospital," they say. "The least God can do is send them a card."

Basically, these people are asking, "Why can't God be as nice as I am?"

"If I was all powerful," they say, "*I* would heal the sick . . . except for people with call-waiting, whom I would smite with boils whenever they put me on hold. Also, drivers in an approaching car who didn't switch off their high beams would get an instant rash."

So maybe we're not all that nice. But we expect God to be. And that's why it's so surprising when He lets us suffer. Every once in a while I get a migraine headache, which feels like a pack of wolverines are gnawing at my brain. I know other people with migraines who bravely go about their daily activities in spite of the eye-squinting pain. I also go about my activities, only my favorite activity involves curling up in the fetal position and whimpering softly to myself, "Please, God, make it stop hurting."

I'm always a little put out that God doesn't heal me immediately. I figure that it's got to be an easy fix for Him. He can restore sight to the blind. How much trouble can a headache be? I'm a baptized, tithe-paying Christian, as well as a two-time champion at Bible Pictionary. Why can't I get a little customer service? Why do I get nothing, and other people get divine help in finding their lost hamsters?

My friend Diane has a different response to suffering. She is both a saint and a skilled shopper. On one of her recent shopping sorties, she found a beautiful pair of cream-colored slacks. They fit perfectly. Her whole life was suffused with the warm glow of this blessing. Then suddenly, tragedy struck. She accidentally sat on a blueberry.

The resources of our great civilization were called upon to remove the stain, and they all failed. As she entered the valley of the shadow, Diane also questioned God. But it was a different kind of question from mine. She asked, "Lord, what lesson do you want me to learn from this?"

There is one aspect of this question that gives me pause. It almost sounds like God is planning every bad thing that happens. This is an accusation normally reserved for members of the opposing political party and ex-husbands.

Of course, people mean it in a good way. It brings comfort to think that God has some higher purpose in allowing an unfortunate event to befall us. Maybe He wanted Diane to learn a valuable lesson about checking for stray pieces of fruit before plopping down in a chair.

But what seems more likely to me is that we have been given free will. And in a world with free will, we find ourselves rowing down the rapids created by our decisions and the decisions of thousands of people around us. Every once in a while, we just hit a rock.

But another aspect to Diane's question does work for me. Doesn't it seem that God enjoys bringing good out of bad situations? Take Joseph as an example. He's tossed in prison because he refused an employee-benefits package offered by his boss's wife. His future looks as grim as a British sci-fi movie. Then, BAM! He becomes Pharaoh's right-hand man, and all the universities want him to come speak at their graduation.

We live in a sinful world, and pain happens. So do poverty, earthquakes, and hairy moles. God could suspend the laws of nature every time we're in danger of getting hurt or embarrassed, but for reasons that are probably too complicated to fit on a bumper sticker, He rarely does.

God can still be trusted. If you give Him a chance, He can bring some redeeming good out of our personal suffering. Meanwhile, take two aspirin and wait for that great gettin' up morning.

"Unclean, Unclean"

You know it's time to do a little housecleaning when you walk across the kitchen and one of your slippers sticks to the floor. Things have gone too far when neighbors write WASH ME on your windows.

At times like these, there is one surefire way to deal with the problem—invite someone over for Sabbath lunch. Nothing motivates *me* to clean house like the fear of people finding out how we really live.

Please understand: my wife and I would *like* to have a tidy house. But after full days at the office we barely have the energy to pronounce simple words, much less dance around the place with a mop and sponge. Our approach to housecleaning is "If I can endure the mess another day, maybe the other person will take care of it."

Lori can always outwait me when it comes to the kitchen garbage. She has a knack for balancing empty bottles, cans, and cereal boxes on an already full container until the garbage towers up like the Matterhorn. She could let the kitchen and half the living room fill up with debris, waiting for me to crack and take it out—which I eventually do.

I, on the other hand, will let the bathroom deteriorate to the point where even a returned missionary would fear to step inside the door. When Lori can't stand it any longer, I see her heading into the master bath wearing rubber gloves and carrying a long-handled brush like someone about to do battle with the Ebola virus.

The wait-and-see method of housecleaning has serious shortcomings as far as the refrigerator is concerned. Sometimes Lori will discover a plastic tub hiding behind the mayo that she's afraid to open. She will leave it on the counter, its sides bulging with toxic gas, in the hope that I will have the courage to unleash whatever living thing breeds inside and chase it into the garbage disposal.

Neighborhood kids in search of a last-minute science project stop by and ask what we have growing in the fridge. It makes me wonder if the cure for the common cold might be evolving right now on last November's macaroni salad.

Of course, everyone has different sanitary standards. In my opinion, premarital counseling should test for cleaning compatibility. It might include a walk through the apartments of each of the betrothed.

"All right, Suzy," the counselor might say. "We see that John is cleaning engine parts in his bathtub. Can you live like this for the rest of your life?"

Or the counselor could ask probing questions of the future bride and groom. "Let's say that a lasagna explodes in your microwave. How long would each of you let this go before cleaning it up?"

If their answers differ by more than seven days, call the wedding off.

Professional testing is necessary because you can't tell the truth about your intended just by visiting their apartment. Remember, when you visit *before* you're married, you are company. Presumably your beloved has tidied up in anticipation of your arrival.

Before our nuptials my wife could only guess that my standards of cleanliness fell somewhere *above* boys at junior camp and *below* our neighbor who won't let his wife do the vacuuming because she doesn't leave perfectly straight lines in the carpet.

After the honeymoon, Lori found out that I have a short attention span for cleaning. I'll be washing dishes, and pretty soon I'll say to myself, "This is not the rewarding experience it was when I began. I think I'll do something else helpful around the house, such as check to make sure the TV remote works properly."

Every so often I make a stab at cleaning up the paper clutter in our house, but then I think, *What's the point?* The U.S. Post Office employs people full-time to drop off a fresh load every day of the week.

I guess that in view of the conflict of the ages, our daily battle against grime and clutter is a trivial thing. The devil might make us feel guilty about the dust bunnies under our bed, but I'm not sure God would. Judging by what Jesus said, it's more important to be clean on the inside.

I don't need to tell you that. No doubt you've prayed David's prayer, "Create in me a clean heart, O God."* Once again, the secret to getting things cleaned up is inviting Someone over.

---

* Psalm 51:10, KJV

My House Runneth Over

I'll tell you when the things of this earth grow strangely dim. It's when you have to move them. After packing your third box of cat toys, you begin to wonder, *Where did all this stuff come from?*

The answer is probably Wal-Mart. You can't go there every week for five years and not end up with some kind of a net gain. First the cabinets fill up, then the closets, then the garage, until the only place left to store your back issues of *National Geographic* is the trunk of the Chevy.

Male or female, none of us can resist getting new stuff any more than we can pass the sample tray at Mrs. Fields. Guys will bring home anything with a motor. For example, my friend Trent once found himself walking out of a store with a battery-powered Tootsie Pop.

While men are drawn to items that have some sort of function, women—and this is the kind of generalization that really should be punishable by a fine or imprisonment—like to be surrounded by stuff that serves no practical purpose.

They like to feather the nest with Precious Moments figurines, matching candlesticks, and pillow shams. (As I understand it, pillow shams are frilly coverings for pillows that make them "too pretty" to actually sleep on, unless you're Louis the XIV.)

Women also like to have their stuff with them on the road. Go to any hotel, and you'll see some poor husband struggling like a Hong Kong coolie with five suitcases, four of which are full of his wife's shoes. His own clothes are probably stuffed into the corner of his shaving kit.

For shorter trips out of the house, women have the purse. Now, in all honesty, if I had to be stranded on an island with only one object, I'd vote for my wife's purse. Food, building materials, medical supplies—it's all in there.

The purse is such a good idea that I think men should have them. Guys could carry their most important possessions with them wherever they went: a roll of duct tape, an economy-size can of WD-40, a twin pack of Nutty Bars, and a softball trophy—in case the summer of '87 ever comes

73

up in casual conversation.

I think the world would be a better place if men carried purses. I can imagine a board meeting where a vice president might say, "Hey, a screw just popped out of my laptop. Does anyone have a 6-millimeter Allen wrench?" Then all the guys around the table would start rummaging through their purses until they found one.

Rummaging may be the biggest downside to purses. I am acquainted with two documented cases of women who carry flashlights to aid in their rummaging.

Apparently, the purse is like this portable closet where you throw everything that will fit. Then when you need one of the items, you have to grope about in the shadowy recesses until you find it, emerging with the same sense of triumph as Stanley returning from the heart of Africa. Only instead of finding Livingstone, you've got a box of Clorets.

Whether we have a purse or not, we all have plenty of stuff. Some of it seems precious. Then I think of those TV interviews with families standing in front of a home leveled by an earthquake or fire. They always say, "Yeah, we lost everything, but that doesn't matter. We're all safe."

When we weigh our relationships against our possessions, there's no contest. The more intense the relationship, the more dramatically it devalues everything around it.

Which is just another way of saying that when you turn your eyes upon Jesus, the things of earth will grow strangely dim in the light of His glory and grace.

No Thanks.
I'm Stuffed.

My wife just got back from the mall, and now I can safely say that we have enough stuff.

Before today an argument could have been made that we needed more stuff. After all, there was a patch of empty space on top of the refrigerator. But now we have reached TSS, or Total Stuff Saturation.

The key indicator of TSS is when you commit to living in the same house for the rest of your life because the idea of packing everything for a move causes your breath to come in short gasps, as it did the time you found out your boss can access all your old e-mails.

Let's imagine that tomorrow I get a phone call from someone saying, "Hey, Kim, we've got a job for you in Hawaii. We'll pay you big money to evaluate the cooking in fine restaurants."

My reply would be "Thanks, but physicists have warned us that moving our stuff will cause the world to tilt out of balance. I wouldn't feel right putting my career above the safety of the planet."

One of the great tensions in our society—besides the tension between our desire to help local schools raise money and our ambivalence about Corbi's pizza—is the tension between wanting more stuff and not having a place to put it. According to the National Association of Home Builders, the size of the average home has increased by 800 square feet since 1970, mostly because people need more room to store their Beanie Baby collection.

My wife accumulates stuff because she's a sentimental soul. She has hung on to her grandmother's cheese grater, a Mormon-sized family of Barbie dolls, and even some old tissues left behind by tearful guests at our wedding.

This makes me think that every home should have a museum wing where you can keep objects from your past. You could give tours and explain, "Here's a display of valentines I received in third grade. Here are Jennifer's old retainers. And this exhibit is dedicated to unflattering pictures of my husband's former girlfriends."

I don't have anything against memorabilia, but I guess what I'm trying to say is this: I don't need any more stuff. This declaration makes me feel strong and unencumbered by the things of this world. (At least until I see a Circuit City; then I can't wait to be encumbered by the latest product from sweet, sweet Sony.)

For a while I thought yard sales would be the answer. I could exchange unwanted stuff around our house for cash, which, unlike a collection of old Avon bottles, is wanted around our house. Then I spent two rainy days at a group yard sale and made $20—half of which I spent buying stuff from other people at the sale.

The battle never ends. There is too much stuff in the world, all of it leaping into our homes like frogs in the Egyptian plague.

Of course, things have changed since the time of the pharaohs. Now we've learned that you can't take it with you. What a relief.

Division of Labor

Let's turn in our Bibles to Genesis 2:18. The Lord God said, "It is not good for man to be alone. I will make a helper for him. Otherwise, the plates will never get put in the dishwasher."

At least that's how it is in our house. I can always find something more interesting to do than scrub dishes. "Well, I hate to eat and run, honey, but I need to read up on this fascinating credit card offer we got in the mail."

My approach to cleaning up the crockery can be summed up in the phrase "Let's let it soak a little longer."

One of the reasons that I endorse marriage as one of God's great ideas—right up there with the opposable thumb and corn on the cob—is that sometimes your spouse will pick up the chores that you detest. If I had known ahead of time that Lori would happily take on the ironing of my shirts, I would have lobbied vigorously to move up our wedding date by six months.

I can hear you saying, "You've got your wife doing the dishes and all the ironing. What exactly do *you* do to help around the house?"

Well, that's a fair question, although I don't appreciate your tone of voice.

I take on my share of the chores. Every six months or so, I change the oil in the car.

Lori's editorial note: Big deal. You drive the car to Jiffy Lube and read their magazines.

And that's not all. I crawl under the house to change the air conditioner filter. I take care of the lawn and the garden, clean the shower, and cook breakfast.

Lori's editorial note: Kim cleans the shower about the time he starts to worry about getting athlete's foot; the "garden" is three tomato plants, if you count the dead one; and "cooking breakfast" involves tossing a Cheerios box on the table.

I also do the taxes.

Lori's editorial note: Yeah, he does do that.

My point is that in a good relationship, you can depend on your partner to take care of certain responsibilities. Then you never have to worry about them again.

I know a delightful couple that has their own way of dividing responsibility. She does all the talking, and he does all the thinking.

She: "So, we had a wonderful weekend of skiing at . . . what was that place called, dear? The place with all the snow?"

He: "Aspen."

She: "And while we were there we saw that movie star. . . . Honey, what was his name?"

He: "Tom Hanks."

Whether we want to admit it or not, we all depend on other people. Even Martha Stewart can't do everything herself. Somebody is washing her car and putting yesterday's dried flower arrangement up in the attic. Which, I suppose, frees her to concentrate on her plan for world domination.

What a relief it is to trust someone to take care of the things you can't seem to do for yourself. I suppose that's the kind of peace that comes in a trusting relationship with God.

When you're facing life's little wrinkles, it helps to know that Someone has promised to take on the ironing.

Waste Not, Why Not?

Here's an interesting statistic: The U.S. produces almost 400 million tons of garbage each year. Most of that is made up of trial-offer CDs for America Online and empty Wal-Mart bags; but still, you've got to admit that we throw away a great deal of stuff.

At work I toss a lot of memos. We have this huge copy machine that works all day and into the night spitting out memos that say something like: "Employees are asked to refrain from bringing iguanas to the office during regular work hours." Distributing 200 memos is seen as preferable to going straight to Julio in accounts payable and telling him that his coworkers are no longer amused when his pet eats their office plants.

I admit to a certain sense of accomplishment when I throw things out because, frankly, we have too much stuff in our house. We have more shoes than the entire nation of Bangladesh. I have no record player but lots of old records, including one featuring Engelbert Humperdinck with a pair of sideburns that would frighten small children. And we have accumulated a great stockpile of Band-Aids, as if our family is in imminent danger of falling into a raspberry bush.

I think my generation is more willing to throw things away than that of my parents. Their generation wouldn't *dream* of throwing out the baby *or* the bathwater. "In the old days we didn't use bathwater just once," says my dad. "The whole neighborhood used the same bathwater. We drew names to see who would go first. If you were in the top 10, you were grateful."

When I was growing up, we never disposed of anything. Margarine tubs served as our breakfast china. Paper towels were all right for the Rockefeller family, but when we needed to wipe up a spill, we used remnants from old pajamas. And don't even get me started on aluminum foil. I remember reusing one 10-inch square through the entire Nixon administration.

In contrast, my generation came up with the disposable razor, the disposable camera, and—after a brief infatuation with tech stocks—we discovered the disposable retirement fund.

I've noticed that the next generation is even better at throwing stuff out than we are. The other day I was trying to take care of an urgent personal entertainment matter, and I couldn't find the DVD remote. My wife recalled some suspicious activity on the part of our 1-year-old, which led me to look in the garbage can. There was the remote.

It turns out that our boy had been amusing himself for about a week by throwing household items into the garbage. Some items we recovered. Others are at the county landfill, including a pair of new shoes.

Our boy was smart enough not to throw out any of his *own* toys—a surprising number of which play chipper pieces of music. I once stumbled into the family room in the dark and simultaneously set off three songs, including a number by Jay Jay the Jet Plane called "Wing Wiggling" and a Barney song in which the purple dinosaur talks about his "need for love."

Human beings resemble that singing Barney doll. We are annoying, needy, and not that bright. By all accounts, sinners like us should have become extinct a long time ago. But God keeps trying to save us, unwilling to dispose of anyone until the last possible minute. No matter how *we* feel about clutter, God seems happiest when His house is full.

Oh, Keys,
Where Art Thou?

One of the benefits of family life is that there are always people around who will respond to your plea "Has anyone seen my keys?" Or, to be more accurate, there is the hope that someone will respond.

In reality, your family members are unable to give your problem the slightest attention because of pressing concerns of their own, such as fingernail hygiene.

I have lost many things, including socks, retainers, and the entire body of learning from my sophomore year of college. But this thing with my keys is starting to wear on my usually sweet disposition.

It's like being forced to play a game of hide-and-seek with myself. My hands drop the keys someplace, next my brain goes off and counts to 100, and then it tries to find the keys.

Now, I can hear someone saying, "Why don't you put your keys in the same place every time?" Well, maybe I *am* putting them in the same place. I just can't remember where that place is.

The good thing about losing your keys is that it can reinvigorate your prayer life. I'm almost surprised that the Lord's Prayer doesn't make a place between "Give us our daily bread" and "forgive us debts" for a little something about "return to us our keys before we're late for work."

Speaking of the heartbreak of personal loss, my wife recently had an incident involving her toothbrush. I wasn't thinking clearly one morning, and I accidentally picked up the wrong toothbrush—*her* toothbrush. Well, let's just say she never used it again. I'm thinking: *We're married! It's not like she's sharing a toothbrush with a viral research monkey.*

My wife also gets upset when she loses receipts. That's because without a receipt she can't return items to the store, and she eventually returns *everything*. From her perspective, a department store serves the same function as a bank. You give them both money. Then they both give you a piece of paper that you use to get the money back. Only the department store is superior because it also gives you a stylish new blouse.

But perhaps I am drifting from my topic, which is basically as follows: People lose things. This is the chief reason that God did not give us removable body parts.

"Hey, Mom. Have you seen my ear?"

"Check the pool filter, honey."

While we are troubled by losing things, finding things is a joy. In fact, some people make a hobby out of finding the things that their fellow human beings have lost. Recently I read an Internet posting by a man with a metal detector who was enthusing about a particularly good day at the beach.

"We found four pennies," he recalls with satisfaction, "and two hotel keys in separate spots, and a large stainless-steel spoon made in Norway."

You get the feeling that if he ever found a quarter, the excitement would give him an aneurysm.

We're happy to gain, and sad to lose. Every bad feeling I can think of is about loss. We're grieving loss or fearing loss or just plain angry about loss. When we are losers, we are weepers.

Jesus proposes to change this. He encourages us to let go of things so that they will no longer have a hold on us.

I recently attended a funeral, and even in the midst of the most painful loss, the agony was blunted by the hope of the resurrection. There is the sense that most of what we are afraid to lose isn't very important, and if it *is* important, it will be restored to us someday with compounded interest.

That is a key to peace of mind that no one can afford to lose.

Gold, Frankincense, and Jumper Cables

Where are some areas in which men just can't compete with women. For one thing, we don't look as good in Capri pants. And for another, we are as far behind women in gift-giving skills as some species of tree fungus.

I have such a record of failure in shopping for Christmas gifts that I've found it's more convenient to give a receipt and leave the actual gift at the store. But my wife makes a yearlong endeavor of choosing Christmas gifts of such variety and splendor that Aladdin comes off like an amateur. Whereas I've never quite figured out the concept of hostess gifts, Lori won't even show up at Motel 6 without a little something for the desk clerk.

I wonder if women do better at giving presents because that's the way God made them. Maybe God gave women the ability to choose a perfect gift for any occasion. And to help even things out, He gave men the ability to back up boat trailers.

You may not be convinced that men are "differently abled" when it comes to giving presents. But you have to admit that it answers a lot of the questions that spring to mind after exchanging gifts with men.

Why do men buy such strange gifts? Men are practical. They often make the mistake of buying something that you actually need—such as garden fertilizer—instead of what you want—which is usually another pair of shoes. This practical bent explains why a distant cousin of mine bought his grandmother a pair of jumper cables for Christmas.

Another reason for giving strange gifts is Vacation Bible School. Every summer, young boys bring their mothers napkin holders made out of Popsicle sticks. When the mothers make a big fuss over receiving these gifts, the boys can be forgiven for thinking, *Hey, you can bring anything to a woman and she'll love it.*

In certain cases, men buy strange gifts because they suffer from gift dyslexia. You can tell if a man has gift dyslexia by giving him this simple test.

A good wedding gift is:

    a. a chain saw

b. a crystal bowl

c. a pet boa constrictor

The correct answer is "b." Or is it "a"? I'm afraid I've lost the answer sheet.

Why do men spend either too much or too little on a gift? It's like poor depth perception. Men have a hard time knowing how much to spend in a certain situation. Generally we try to err on the high side. A good example of that is King Ahasuerus in the Bible. When Esther made her entrance, he said, "What is thy request? It shall be given thee up to half of my kingdom." Here was a man who didn't know how much to spend on a gift but wasn't about to get caught short.

My friend Doug has developed a clever way to cope with his poor price perception. When he opens an anniversary gift from his wife, he quickly judges its value. If it costs more than what he spent, he waits until she opens her present, and then he says ". . . *and* I'm taking you out to dinner!"

Why do men always wait until the last minute to buy gifts? The answer to this question is simple: Men hate to shop. Most of us would rather run naked through an Iraqi minefield than spend an hour in Sears looking for that "special something." So we shop late and we shop fast.

On Christmas Eve in our town you'll find my boss literally trotting through the mall in search of a present for his wife. When it comes to getting a wrapped present under the tree, he takes pride in having a faster delivery time than Domino's Pizza.

Why do men buy the same gifts year after year? Once we find a gift that makes a woman happy, we cling to it like Velcro. A man who knows what to buy his wife on every one of her birthdays until the Second Coming is a man who is supremely confident about the future.

I think of a family friend who discovered he could be a hit with his wife if he gave her Wedgwood china. On every gift-giving occasion he would deliver a new place setting. Many years later, the poor man was crushed when his wife suggested he try a new gift idea. "I think that 75 place settings is adequate for most of our entertaining," she said gently.

* * *

I hope these insights into how men buy gifts will make you more sympathetic and forgiving as you sneak their gifts back to the store for a cash refund.

I wonder which of us has the greatest advantage in the Christian life. Maybe it's women, who seem to know more perfectly the joy of giving. Or maybe it's men, who are more acquainted with grace in the sense that even when we have little to offer, we are still loved.

Paying Mother Back

Be sure to mark your calendar for Mother's Day a day when we honor mothers for making their biggest contribution to society—ourselves.

If someone is responsible for your existence on the planet, the least you can do is buy them a card.

Moms never seem bothered by the inequity between what they give (life) and what they get (14 lines of Helen Steiner Rice, and if they're lucky, burnt toast in bed). If mothers ever started pushing for a better return on their investment, we'd be in trouble: "You know, dear, you weren't able to feed yourself for 10 months after you were born. Could you watch my cats for a couple weeks?"

My point is: moms don't ask for much. All they want is for you to keep your room clean, dress nicely for church, and graduate from medical school.

If you haven't done these things already, you might want to consider them as a way to make this Mother's Day more special.

Here are some other ideas:

Serve her breakfast in bed. Perhaps the best thing about keeping mom in bed is that she can't see what you're doing to her kitchen. Anyway, it's a nice gesture.

Reduce her guilt. Mothers often fear that they made mistakes in raising their children that warped them for life. You would do your mother a great favor if you convinced her that you are warped for reasons completely beyond her control. For example, I tell my mom to consider all those spills I took on my bicycle before the popularity of helmets. You can also blame all the Play-Doh you ate or the time you stumbled on a copy of *Fox's Book of Martyrs* at age 8.

Bury the pain of the past. Many of us were raised during the golden age of corporeal punishment. Teachers drilled holes in long, wooden paddles to reduce wind resistance and gave them pet names such as "Teacher's Little Helper."

On the home front moms found 100 creative ways to follow Solomon's advice—reaching for flyswatters, flip-flops, the *Ladies' Home Journal,* and whatever else fell to hand to make sure we wouldn't be spoiled. My workmate Cassandra says that her mother used a wooden spoon on her bottom so consistently that she didn't even know it was for cooking.

These days, the controversy over spanking is pricking the conscience of some mothers, so it is very important to say with a perfectly straight face that you appreciate the fact that she loved you enough to whack the stuffing out of you. Tell her that spankings taught you the difference between right and wrong. (They also taught you to never buy those paddleball toys because they can come back to haunt you.)

Let your mother think you've amounted to something. It's very important to mothers that those umpteen hours of agony in the delivery room will come to good, and not evil. So Mother's Day is a good time to remind them of your successes and achievements during the past year.

For example, show Mom the personalized letter you received from Ed McMahon. Casually mention that you've qualified for a gold MasterCard. And if you've won an Emmy for daytime television, don't be embarrassed. Tell her about that, too. The funny thing about a mother's love is that she will rejoice with you in even your smallest victories

Which, I suppose, is God's attitude. He rejoices at even our smallest accomplishments in the Christian life.

But this is no reason to get a big head and think we're paying Him back for all He's done for us. It's like Mother's Day. There are some little things we can do to show our appreciation, But in the end we're still the indebted and grateful child.

Write a Quickie
Christmas Letter

Who came up with the idea of sending Christmas letters? Is it possible that this individual didn't have enough to do during the holidays?

I'm trying to imagine someone saying, "I've gone shopping, hosted the office party, decorated the tree, attended the school play, practiced for the church pageant, and baked cookies for the boss. I might as well send 50 letters to people I haven't seen since polyester pantsuits."

Well, let us not be distracted by our feelings of resentment toward this person. He or she will be dealt with on judgment day. For now our task is to write a Christmas letter as quickly and easily as possible.

Follow this handy template, and you can dash one off in the time it takes most people to remember which verse comes after "10 lords a-leaping."

Part A: The Salutation. If you plan to photocopy your letter, it's best to go with a generic greeting such as "Dear Friends" or "Dear Sentient Being." Creative people are able to come up with a single greeting that captures their sentiments about all the people on their mailing list. One example might be: "Dear snobs who never gave me the respect I deserved until I married a neurosurgeon."

Part B: The Opening. Always begin with the words "I can't believe how quickly this year has passed." Then give the reason that time has passed so swiftly, such as "Because we've been so busy on the ranch" or "Because I was in a coma for eight months."

Part C: News and Accomplishments. As I see it, there are two types of people on your mailing list. First there are those who love you and rejoice in your successes (your mother). Then there are those who feel threatened by your achievements and would like to see you brought down a notch (everybody else).

So rest assured that you're not pleasing the majority of your readers when you throw a line like this in your letter: "Herb's business has doubled in the past year, and you would laugh to see the crazy ideas our tax accountant has to hide our staggering income."

No, if you really want to hold the attention of your audience, write: "You should see how much weight Herb has put on. I took one of his suits to the cleaner last week, and they said, 'We don't do curtains.'"

Part D: The Kids. This is the part where you brag about your children. Take a few sentences to list their accomplishments. Perhaps Jennifer graduated from dental school. Or maybe Clem, Jr., was granted early parole. Obviously, this part of the letter will vary from child to child.

Part E: The Invitation. As you near the end of the letter, it is appropriate to invite your readers to visit you if they are ever in your area. Now, I always wish this part of the letter were more specific. Is it an invitation to stay overnight? How big is the bed in their guest room? Do they accept pets? Do they get cable?

On our Christmas letters this year I intend to come right out and say that we have a three-night maximum stay—four nights if the guests do some light yard work.

Of course, we'd rather have our friends and kinfolk visit us than receive a letter. But they live too far away. So a letter is the best way to be known and remembered and understood by these special people.

Perhaps our spiritual distance from God is the reason we hardly ever hear from Him except in letters. Fortunately, we have the Bible as evidence that God also wants to be known and remembered and understood.

Listen to Your Mother

As we approach National Maybe-a-Card-Will-Make-Mom-Feel-Better-About-Another-Year-of-Being-Stuck-With-the-Dishes-Day, I feel we should take a moment to recognize Uncle Arthur. While not an actual mother himself, he was sympathetic to their plight and did more than any person since Moses to persuade us to honor our mothers.

In case you were raised by wolves in Siberia, I should mention that Uncle Arthur wrote a series of books called *Bedtime Stories*. Each volume contained dozens of true anecdotes about boys with names like Bobby and girls with names like Susan. What generally happened was that Bobby or Susan would neglect to obey their mother, and then—WHAM—something awful would happen to them. Susan's stubbornness would result in her brand-new watch being ruined, or Bobby's rambunctious behavior would cause the town to be trampled by a herd of wildebeest.

Naturally, parents embraced the idea that disobeying them was the root cause of pestilence, plague, and personal tragedy. They bought Uncle Arthur's books by the bazillions. Then they read the stories to us impressionable children as we hovered in the hypnotic state of early sleep. Into our vulnerable brains would waft the message that if we obeyed our moms, we would not be buried under a crashing mountain of jam jars, like little Jimmy when he tried to sneak a forbidden treat (volume 4, page 46).

Did it work? Of course it did. I still feel a sense of impending danger if I find a jam jar in an overhead cabinet. As for obeying my mother, well . . .

Have you ever thought of how life might have been different if you *had* listened to your mom? You would be able to play the clarinet. You would have avoided that unpleasant relationship with the person with the tattoo. And you would be remembered by your high school classmates for wearing a conservative style of dress most commonly associated with the cast of *Oklahoma!*

Deep down inside we all know it's right to submit to a mother's instruction. We also know we should cut back on fossil fuels and cheesecake, but we don't do that, either.

Mothers are wiser and more experienced in every significant area of life, including love, politics, and stain removal. So why don't we listen? We choose instead to listen to our playmates, who, judging from the way they break into giggles when we fall down and injure ourselves, probably don't have our best interests at heart.

The one time we pay attention to Mom is when we're in trouble. We won't listen to her admonition to practice the piano, but after a disastrous recital, we want to hear her exclaim that she is still proud of us and that we *really* are very talented. Our ears are tuned to another station when she tells us not to run with a sharp stick, but she has our complete attention when we need help pulling the stick out of our little brother.

I think God must sympathize closely with mothers. He's older and wiser and more experienced than anyone, and still He gets only a grudging amount of attention. Look in the Bible, and you see all these stories that sound a lot like Uncle Arthur's. Jonah disobeys God and ends up as a salty snack for a whale. Paul starts bullying God's people and ends up looking for his contacts on the road to Damascus. Samson ignores God and becomes a piñata at Philistine parties.

So when will we listen?

When we trust God more than ourselves. Sometimes it takes a lot of time and a lot of digging out from under the jam jars before that happens—before we learn to listen to the voice of the One who loves us most.

Merry Christmas.
Now Go Home.

A ny day now you'll turn on the radio and hear "You better watch out . . . Santa Claus is coming to town." The same could be said for relatives.

The holidays require that you fill the house with kinfolk who will all pop out of bed just 30 seconds before you do and hit the showers, ensuring that you won't see the inside of a bathroom until after lunch. These are people with a natural instinct for getting on your nerves. Only a relative will raise one eyebrow and say, "Is *that* what you're wearing to church?" Only a relative will say, "Nice mustache, Mom."

I try to do my part to reduce tension by keeping my holiday visits short. I've found that when relatives greet me at the airport, their feelings of goodwill are running at a peak. But if too many days go by with me asking "What's for dinner?" and "When are you going to put more gas in the car?" goodwill becomes less of a feeling and more of a place where people drop off unwanted furniture.

So how do you know when you've stayed too long? That's a tough question, because relatives feel guilty about telling you straight out. I've learned to look for subtle hints, such as (1) You find airplane tickets in your cereal bowl; (2) Your host says he needs the guest room because a friend is about to get out on parole; (3) Your host pauses during worship and wonders out loud if Daniel's 2,300-day prophecy might also apply to your visit.

As long as you're staying with relatives, though, it's best to take their little quirks in stride. Otherwise you might find that even the *way* they open Christmas presents can be annoying. Cheri told me how her in-laws have turned exchanging gifts into such a regulated and unending process that it resembles Chinese water torture.

Gifts must be opened one at a time, each person taking their turn. Care must be exercised in preserving the wrapping paper, using a knife to cut along the tape. After the gift is revealed, a few moments are allowed for exclamations of surprise and wonder, followed by the gift-giver saying, "If you don't like it, you can take it back." In homes with a mess of grandkids, this ritual can take longer than the announcements at camp meeting.

Sometimes a little friction will arise over how *much* to spend on presents. I've discovered that you can try to say "No gift over $5." But the minute you're out of the room, Grandma is giving little Jessica the complete Barbie subdivision with remote control car. Soon relatives are pulling expensive gifts out of their hiding places, and you look pretty cheap for giving everyone new ice-cube trays.

Oh, it sounds like I'm being a Scrooge. Actually, I love getting together with relatives, and I love Christmas. If it wasn't for Christmas, I'd never have any new socks.

Of course, it's also a beautiful reminder of the first Advent. I think Jesus appreciates us celebrating His birth.

And right now, as He prepares heavenly mansions for us, the watching universe is saying, "Are you sure you want to invite those humans for such a long stay? You know how annoying they can be."

"What can I do?" Jesus will say with a smile only a human can understand. "They're my relatives."

Surprise Me

C hristmas is just around the corner—that wonderful time of year when families get together to exchange both gifts and the flu virus.

I hope I didn't cause any of you to panic as you realize that you still have 37 names to go on your Christmas list and the only way you can finish shopping on time is to quit your day job and park your camper at the mall.

Christmas used to be simpler. The toughest thing about shopping was finding some shiny apples for the children's stockings.

If you want to make a gift of an apple these days, it better have 2 gigs of RAM and a flat-screen monitor. Today's young people come up with wish lists that bear a striking resemblance to the inventory records of Best Buy.

But that's what makes it easy to shop for kids—they're not shy about telling you what they want, sometimes even renting billboards along your route to work, or making impassioned speeches about the critical role of new in-line skates to their future welfare and self-esteem.

Adults are more cagey. Especially mothers, who will say things such as, "You don't have to buy me anything this year. It's enough that you're spending Christmas with me. What more can I ask for than the privilege of cooking for you and cleaning up after you?"

If you have someone like this on your gift list—someone who is not forthcoming with any ideas—let me suggest an item I saw in the Sharper Image catalog. I refer to the Electric Tongue Cleaner, priced at a reasonable $30, with a long, slim design that "makes it easy to clean the important area far back on your tongue." (Battery is not included.)

Give one of those, and the next time you ask the recipient what they want for Christmas, I guarantee that you will get answers!

Actually, my own wife will not tell me what she wants for Christmas. This, no doubt, is a result of my deeply held belief that the best gifts are a surprise.

In our early years of marriage Lori would say, "I'd love to have a new vacuum cleaner for Christmas."

And I would respond, "Well, *now* I can't get that for you, because it wouldn't be a surprise."

Soon Lori learned to ask me only for things she *doesn't* want. "I could sure use another pair of Isotoner gloves," she'll say.

I know I'm not the only one who values the element of surprise. I'm thinking of Melanie, who married into a family whose chief preholiday amusement involves guessing what gifts are coming their way. They are not above shaking presents, sleuthing through closets, or peeking into shopping bags.

Every time one of her purchases is discovered, though, Melanie insists on returning it to the store, often with an in-law close behind saying, "But I really *wanted* that." One year she had to buy a new present three times for the same relative.

In my mind, surprising gifts contain elements of the divine. When we bring our desires to our heavenly Father, He often asserts His privilege to surprise us—to give us something better than we asked for. Or to deliver what we asked for in an unexpected way.

If you want someone who will simply deliver the items on your wish list, then you're not looking for God. You're looking for Santa Claus.

What Do Men Want?

Today we will address the question "What do men want for Christmas?" Now, I can hear many women saying, "Who cares what men want? What they need are some new clothes."

This attitude may seem harsh, but we men have brought it on ourselves because we never buy clothes on our own. Some men would not enter a clothing store to escape a cloud of killer bees. So women have taken the initiative, realizing that if not for their efforts, many of us would still be wearing pale-green leisure suits.

Of course, there is another reason men get wardrobe items for Christmas. No matter what a woman *starts* shopping for, she always ends up among the clothing racks. It's an instinctive move, like turning your tithe envelope upside down in the offering plate. A woman will go out for office supplies and end up at Bloomingdale's buying a new pantsuit. When God created woman, it was another way of saying, "Let there be a textile industry."

So the man in your life will be getting something with an elastic waistband for Christmas. That's settled. But what if you also want to get him something special—something that will make his eyes sparkle with joy for a full minute before he starts glancing back at the football game on television?

Perhaps I can help.

The first thing you must remember is that you cannot find out what a man really wants by asking him. You see, as we get older, we men take pride in not wanting *anything* for Christmas. This is in marked contrast to our childhood years, when we begged our parents for everything in the Sears Wish Book, including the Suzy Bake Oven.

Maturity brings a sense of self-sufficiency: we don't need road directions from the gas station attendant, and we don't need new socks because the holes in the old ones are mostly covered by our shoes. It's interesting that a man can feel smug in his self-sufficiency at the same moment he is asking you what's for supper.

Anyway, the things men really want for Christmas fall into two categories.

1. Metal things. Men are fascinated by metal in the same way that women are fascinated by fabric. This explains why the only clothing item that really interests men is the belt buckle.

Some examples of gifts men appreciate that have a high metal content include: hammers, golf putters, and the Porsche 911 Turbo. The Porsche also fits into the second category, which is:

2. Things with motors. My suggestion is to take whatever you currently plan to give your man for Christmas and, if it doesn't already have a motor, add one. For example, a man might be offended if you present him with a pair of nose-hair clippers. But give him *electric* nose-hair-clippers and he'll be so excited he'll take them to work to show his boss.

Well, those are my shopping tips for Christmas.

But if you end up getting the old boy a pair of loose-fitting Dockers, that's OK. Even if the men in your life aren't begging for new pants, they still need them.

God Himself seems to believe that everyone can use some new clothes. Isaiah says: "My soul rejoices in my God. For he has clothed me with garments of salvation and arrayed me in a robe of righteousness."

With gifts like that, we will have a merry Christmas indeed.

★ Isaiah 61:10

Thanks, or No Thanks

I 'm in a good mood. It's one of those lazy Sunday afternoons, and as I cast my eye out the window, I feel nothing but goodwill toward my fellow man and gratitude for —"HEY! GET YOUR DOG OFF MY LAWN."

As I was saying, I'm feeling a surge of gratitude. At the moment I'm thankful for hot showers. Take away the hot shower, and you'll see your community's standards of personal cleanliness drop so fast you'd think you were back in junior camp. Soon you could go out for an evening at the symphony and discover that even the elite of society smell vaguely like the monkey house at the zoo.

I'm also thankful for electric screwdrivers, the whole concept of cotton, and chewable vitamin C.

But I don't have to feel grateful if I don't want to. As a holiday, Thanksgiving is inevitable. But as a sentiment, it is entirely optional.

You can express thanksgiving for fresh raspberries—or you can complain about those nasty little seeds that get stuck between your teeth. You can despair that your teenager causes so much trouble—or you can be thankful that he doesn't get it from your side of the family. You can mourn the fact that you can't afford a pair of Ferragamo slingbacks—or you can be thankful that your husband doesn't know how many shoes you already own.

If you look at it the right way, everything gives you the option of being grateful (with the exception of cholera outbreaks and those little stickers they put on fruit).

I saw this principle demonstrated the other day at an emergency room. A coworker was waiting to see his daughter who had just been brought in from a car wreck. When he saw her, he was thankful on two levels. First, he was grateful that she'd sustained no injuries serious enough to rate a mention in their Christmas newsletter. Second, he hoped that the accident would scare her into being the most careful motorist since *Driving Miss Daisy*.

This "give thanks in all things"★ attitude is also evident in one of my relatives, who was forced as a young man to take up housekeeping in a 1972 Chevy pickup.

"Sure, it was cold, cramped, and hygienically challenged," he says. "And it took a broad-minded woman to consider a date with me. But on the other hand, there were no responsibilities and no bills. I had maximum mobility and plenty of fresh air."

It also occurs to me that you would never be out of reach of your snacks, you'd have only six square feet of carpet to vacuum, and all you'd have to do to redecorate is hang a new air freshener on the rearview mirror.

So I'm trying to be thankful in all circumstances. And I guess I can be thankful for all kinds of people—even for the neighbor whose idea of walking the dog appears to be bringing the creature to my side of the property line.

I may not feel very grateful for him now, but I always have the option.

★ See 1 Thessalonians 5:18.

Many Happy Returns

Christmas is over. So right now you're either thankful for the gifts bestowed upon you by loved ones—or you're thankful for the liberal return policy at Wal-Mart.

I am reminded of the two freedoms that make America great: (1) that anyone is free to invent a product like the Salad Shooter and market it on nationwide TV as the perfect gift, creating the impression that everyone desperately needs an electrical appliance that hurls bits of radish around the kitchen; (2) that if someone gives you a Salad Shooter for a gift, you are free to return it for a cash refund.

Few people know that the manufacture of Salad Shooters ended in the late 1980s. Since then, though, the cycle of buying and returning them has kept store shelves fully stocked.

If you are considering taking gifts back to the store, I would like to make an observation—you are probably a woman. Men hate to return *anything*. We feel it is our manly obligation to stand by our gift.

No matter that we haven't worn pants that size since sixth grade. As long as the pants have been committed into our care, we will protect them and shelter them in a corner of the closet until we die.

While women are more willing to approach the returns desk, they must first give careful consideration to the complex implications of such a move—much like a presidential decision to invade a foreign country, or my wife's selection of which shoes to wear to church.

Consideration 1: How will the gift giver react to the return? My family runs the whole gamut, from one unnamed relative—who considers it a stain on her personal honor if you return her gift—to another, who begs you to return her present before you've even taken the wrapping off. "Let's drive over to the store now," she insists.

Consideration 2: Is it even *possible* to return the gift? My brother once received a gold Rolex watch as a present from my mother—which was very nice, except that I had never seen gold rust before. We now suspect that she buys all her Christmas gifts from Mexican pushcart vendors. Let me just say that shopping establishments with wheels rarely have a return policy.

Consideration 3: Will you get cash or store credit? Does it really *matter* if you have a $20 credit in the Muffin Pan Store?

Fortunately, most stores shell out cash when you come traipsing back with their merchandise. Deep down they can't be happy about this. They would rather keep your money and let you keep the cabbage steamer or the electric flossing appliance.

It must have taken courage for store owners to begin to offer a return policy. How can you win by giving people their money back?

Sometimes I wonder why God has such a generous return policy. Everyone God redeems is free to return to sin. The option can be exercised any time.

The devil, on the other hand, does his best to block any attempts to return to a good life.

So how can God win when He has such a generous return policy? His only chance is that we'll realize that His gifts are worth keeping.

Cool and Cute:
The Cornerstones of Gift Giving

Are you looking for a gift for that special someone? Do you hope to find just the perfect item that will cause them to gasp with delight and throw their arms around you with an expression that says, "How is it possible that you have discerned the deepest needs of my soul?" If that's the kind of reaction you want, then I suggest you give cash.

However, if you insist on a more personal gift, follow these four shopping tips.

Tip 1: When it comes to buying Christmas gifts for children, never, never, never deviate from a child's wish list. When you're a kid, you do not welcome creativity. You have a list of 20 toys that you need only slightly less than oxygen, and the pool of gift-giving relatives is not large enough for someone to wander off the script and show up on Christmas Eve with an educational game and the economy pack of Hane's underwear. If you're not sure what's on a child's wish list, remember that many children post their lists on the Internet.

Tip 2: If you need a present for a guy, find something that can be described as "cool." An example would be a GPS. A GPS is an amazing electronic device that uses satellites to report your exact location on earth to within 50 feet. Unfortunately, it does not give you this information in any useful way, such as "You are within 50 feet of an excellent donut shop." Instead, it gives you two numbers signifying longitude and latitude, which may have helped Amelia Earhart but mean absolutely nothing to me. Still, every guy who has one agrees that it is very "cool."

Other cool gifts for men include any power tool that is capable of causing serious bodily injury, cowboy boots, and a 1963 split-window Stingray.

Tip 3: If you are shopping for a woman, the operative word is "cute." I say this because I've observed that the highest words of praise that can come out of a woman's lips are "Isn't that cute!"

If something isn't cute to begin with, women will make it cute. As an experiment, I would like to put a woman–preferably a Longaberger basket representative–in charge of a maximum security men's prison. Within three months I bet the place would look like the inside of a Cracker Barrel. All the bunks would have Laura Ashley sheets and pillow shams. Bowls of potpourri would decorate the weight room, and inmates who refused to wallpaper their cells would be kicked out of their Creative Memories class.

One of the best places to find cute gift ideas is in the Lillian Vernon catalog. It includes such items as the birdfeeder angel cat—a garden accessory designed by a cat lover who would apparently like to revise our current understanding of celestial beings.

Now, some of you more crafty women can make your own cute gifts. You have my respect. But you must be strong and resist the temptation to share a handmade craft with a man. No offense, but you're not going to be able to make something a man wants for Christmas—unless you are an electrical engineer or Mrs. Fields.

Tip 4: Well, I hate to add a new name to your shopping list, but what about God? The day of bringing sacrificial animals is pretty much over, so, once again, cash seems like the best choice. At least until you read Micah 6:8, where God writes down His wish list. He says He wants you "to act justly and to love mercy and to walk humbly with your God."

Cool, huh?

Christmas Questions

As a service to you, my readers, I would like to dedicate this column to answering questions about the Christmas holiday. As a further service, I will also make up the questions.

Question 1: "Good gravy! Is it Christmas already! Where has the time gone?"

Recently a group of physicists discovered that time really does go somewhere. A complex set of calculations proves that time moves away from individuals and accumulates at airports. This explains why travelers suddenly find that a one-hour layover can last for six hours or more.

Question 2: "Should we celebrate Christmas? Isn't it pagan in origin?"

I can't imagine that the pagans celebrated Christmas, because the shopping wasn't any good back then. In any case, I try to be open-minded about holidays that inspire my coworkers to bring me cookies.

Question 3: "How can I save money this Christmas?"

Let me point you to the example of my friend Richard. One Christmas Eve he cheerfully dragged home a tree that he had found in a ditch. "Can you believe that they were finished with it already?" he told his wife in amazement.

Question 4: "Wouldn't it be great if they discovered a copyright forbidding any musician from playing 'The Twelve Days of Christmas'?"

Yes.

Question 5: "Are Christmas letters biblical?"

No. Have you noticed that out of all the epistles written by the apostle Paul, none of them are Christmas letters? Can you even imagine what that would be like?

Greetings, fellow believers:

It's been an exciting year for the Paul family. We took a few weeks to visit John on Patmos Island, where we enjoyed the sun and surf.

Otherwise, things are very busy at work, where I feel like I'm chained to my desk. We're very proud of Paul, Jr., who just graduated from Loma Lyra Medical School. Little sister Phoebe, who has a beautiful singing voice, got a thumbs-up at the coliseum. Have a merry Christmas, and we sincerely hope that *your* children will turn out as nice as ours.

Question 6: "How can I have a storybook Christmas this year?"

As anyone who has read a good Christmas story can tell you, the most important ingredients of a wonderful, heartwarming holiday are (1) poverty, and (2) disease.

The best Christmas stories begin with a family that is so poor that they boil old gum wrappers to make soup. The hardworking mother knits socks for the family from pocket lint that she collects from kindly strangers. In the evening Dad gathers the children around the dim light of their last candle. "Things are really slow in the dental floss recycling business," he says. "I'm afraid there won't be any presents this year."

Doesn't this sound like a great story? You've probably already gone to find a hanky.

I once visited a Bible study class in which everyone shared a favorite Christmas memory. And do you know what? The best stories were rooted in poverty.

One woman told about a Christmas when her husband was going to school on the GI bill. They literally didn't have a nickel to spare, so they agreed that they wouldn't exchange gifts. But on Christmas Day her husband surprised her with an electric toaster. Where had he found the money? After much probing, she got him to admit that he'd skipped lunch for a week at the university diner to save the price of the toaster.

That is the magic—no, wait. Magic is too pagan a word. That is the mystery and wonder and grace of Christmas: That out of poverty comes beauty. That out of the cold weather comes family warmth. That out of a stable comes a King.

SECTION 6:

Why Develop character when You can be one?

Trying My Patience

Humans can be annoying. Which is why many people prefer the company of cats.

Cats do not ring you up in the middle of supper and try to sell you a new long-distance telephone plan. Cats do not make clicking noises with their false teeth. Cats do not have call-waiting. Cats do not insist on practicing the clarinet while you're trying to read. And finally, cats do not equip their homes with burglar alarms that go off accidentally while they are on vacation.

Perhaps it would be a more blissful existence if you could limit your social contacts to cats. But this is not possible. In the first place, cats are not that excited about social contact. And second, you will at least have to interact with your family members, who are all too human.

If someone tapes over your Princess Diana TV special, you can be sure it was a family member. And if you're wondering who wolfed down the last of the Special K when you need it to make a potluck roast, there is no point in blaming it on the Democrats. It was probably someone in your own household.

Hard as it may be to believe, my wife has even found a reason to be annoyed with *me*. Apparently, it is a practice in most civilized countries to rinse the dishes and put them in the dishwasher after a meal. I'm a bit lax in following this procedure—which is not a big deal unless we have Cream of Wheat for breakfast.

Cream of Wheat is a scientific wonder. In its natural state this wholesome food hardly needs any chewing. But once it dries inside a cereal bowl, it acquires the characteristics of concrete. To get it off requires either an industrial jackhammer or a 40-day soak in scalding water.

Of course, the people you live with don't mean to be annoying. It's just that they aren't as considerate as you might hope. Basically you want them to be like those English butlers who always show up holding your socks the minute you're ready to put them on.

Instead of discovering that your child has just finished a crayon mural on his bedroom wall, you would no doubt prefer to hear, "I beg your pardon, Mother, but I took the liberty of polishing the family silver in preparation for tomorrow's company."

Jesus said that the poor will be with us always. But He could have said the same about the annoying. There will always be people along your walking route with dogs that "don't bite," but show a great deal more enthusiasm for your ankles than for Alpo. There will be next-door neighbors whose teenage children don't have quite enough ambition to mow the lawn, but just enough to start a garage band. And there will always be a family member who will use a kitchen spice and not put it back in alphabetical order.

Fortunately, God has considered the problem of what to do about the slow, the inconsiderate, and the conceited. He provides the solution among the fruits of the Spirit—the gift of patience.

I think this gift includes the realization that we also have tried the patience of others. That we have been slow, or inconsiderate, or conceited, or that we have left Cream of Wheat in our cereal bowls.

Grace allows us to suffer fools gladly, and even to endure our own foolishness until it is swallowed up in glory.

Note: I especially appreciate the patience of my teachers. Let me say for the record, "You were right, Mr. Wyche. The snake was *not* funny."

It's Not Low Self-esteem;
It's High Humility

Being born in Kansas, I got a head start on humility. That's because Kansas doesn't have the reasons for pride that other states have. New York has the Statue of Liberty. California has the mighty redwood trees. Kansas has the . . . well, it has the Heritage Underwear Show. If they get a request from a tour group, several elderly residents of Junction City will present a pageant of underwear from the 1800s. Obviously, this has not had the theatrical success of *Cats*.

On the one occasion when the citizens of Kansas thought they had something to brag about, it didn't work out. Back in the sixties we had the world's largest ball of twine. It measured 40 feet in circumference and was started by a man named Frank Stoeber, who—I'm guessing—had a great deal of time on his hands and poor TV reception. But then a man in Texas made a bigger ball of string, and our hopes for a twine-ball tourist industry collapsed.

If it were up to us, those of us from Kansas would prefer not to be humble. But since we don't have much choice, we've become very good at it. If the Olympics had a humility event, we would win every time.

"Johnson begins her compulsories by insisting that she doesn't deserve the gold medal as much as her Russian opponent. The honor of being invited to the games is enough for her. And regarding that time when she saved the Guttensohnn quints by performing CPR on all five babies at once, please don't mention it. She says she was only doing what anyone would do in the same situation. The judges are turning in their scores . . . and they are giving her a 9.7!"

Sometimes humility has nothing to do with your heritage. It just happens. Like when you invite the new family at church to a picnic, and the egg salad sandwiches continue to be a topic of discussion several hours later in the ER. Or when you arrive at a social event only to discover that you're the only one who thought it was a costume party.

Humiliation comes in different ways to men and women. Women

seem to feel shame at the slightest possibility of poor etiquette.

"I feel bad that I didn't bring a housewarming gift."

"But you only stopped by to pick up your Avon order, and you've been here a dozen times."

"I still feel bad. Do you like my purse? Please take it."

If men expressed shame in the same way as women, the corporate world would be a very different place. Board meetings would open with the CEO saying, "I feel really, really bad that our profits are down. Let the official minutes reflect that I could use a hug."

Men *do* express shame, but only in situations of absolutely no relevance to real life. If you've ever seen a man miss a six-foot putt on the golf course, you know what I mean. It is the kind of wailing and gnashing of teeth that is normally associated with war refugees.

It just goes to show that the feeling of shame can be as detached from reality as the photos on eHarmony.

Humility is different from shame. Humility is less of a feeling and more of a reality check. It is admitting that just because we can get people to stand when we lead song service, we don't necessarily have a gift for leadership. That just because we're in the parade, it isn't in our honor. And that just because we can dress ourselves in the morning, we may still need God's help with the rest of the day. We all need to be reminded of these things from time to time—even if we're from Kansas.

Join My Judging Ministry

I am willing to judge people. This is a service I provide without charge. People can come to me, and in just a few minutes, I can let them know where they fall short of my standards and the steps they can take to conform to my expectations.

I don't even need to meet a person face-to-face to judge them. For example, I can judge you as you read this column. No offense, but wouldn't your time be better used by cleaning up the kitchen?

So you may be asking me, "Why are you willing to take time out of your busy schedule to provide this service for the public?"

Why? Because I care. I want to do my part to make the world a better place. And if I can do that by pointing out your flaws . . . well, I'm just glad I can give something back to the community.

For example, you may be driving too slow. I'm happy to bring that fact to your attention with a helpful toot of the horn. Or let's say I disagree with your method of disciplining children. I'm happy to point out the areas where you are being too lax. For years people said that they found my point of view particularly "fresh" because it had not been biased by the actual experience of having children of my own.

Now, you may be wondering, *How can I get involved in this ministry?* I'll tell you, it's easier than you think. We each have been given, in a larger or lesser degree, the gift of discernment when it comes to other people's defects.

I, for example, can tell when people use the word "hopefully" incorrectly in a sentence. Because I've been given this special gift, I feel obligated to point out the mistake when I overhear it in a conversation at a restaurant or in a store. You might be surprised by the shocking lack of appreciation that some people show when I offer them assistance in their grammar. (I didn't think people were supposed to hit you if you wore glasses.)

You may think, *How will I find time for a judging ministry with my busy schedule?* Yes, you'll have to give up a portion of the time you spend minding your own business. But this ministry comes with rich rewards.

Judging has an invigorating effect on your self-esteem. You can almost get to the place where you forget about your own shortcomings if you take time to focus on the faults of others. It's a good, good feeling when you realize that, hey, at least you're not as bad as other people.

For example, you possess a great deal of integrity compared to that city councilman who took bribes from the garbage company. Of course, some of the vendors you order from at the office *do* send you some mighty nice gifts. But in that case, it's just the spirit of Christmas.

I hope you will consider taking up a judging ministry of your own. Right now someone you know is doing something wrong. Let them know it hasn't escaped your attention.

By the way, step over here a little closer. Is that a speck in your eye?

Go Make Yourself Useful

Have you noticed how some people lead useful, productive lives? And then there are others who are the human equivalent of a pillow sham? People in the first group are healing the sick, educating children, and building houses. People from the second group are wondering, "What bugs shall we make them eat in our next episode of *Fear Factor?*"

I think we all want to lead a useful life. At least until it's time to wash the dishes, and then we want someone else to be useful. This is why 20 percent of people end up doing 80 percent of the work—an arrangement that works out pretty well as far as the 80 percent are concerned.

But the downside for the 80 percent is that eventually they have to pause and take stock of their lives. I was doing that the other day and realized that my contributions to society pretty much ended in fourth grade, when I participated in a play promoting dental hygiene.

"Honey," I said to my wife the other day, "I feel as though my life is useless. I'm basically a flesh paperweight."

"Ah, sweetheart," she replied, "that's not true. You've done lots of things."

"Like what?"

"Well . . . ah . . . it doesn't matter. I love you anyway. If you lift your feet, I'll vacuum under your chair."

I think men are particularly driven to feel useful. They yearn to be effective on a grand scale—like heading the office committee that reassigns parking spaces.

I think this yearning explains why Stephen Covey sold millions of copies of his book *The 7 Habits of Highly Effective People.* Of course, only about a dozen men actually read the whole book. The rest were halfway into chapter three when they were distracted by the NASCAR season.

I myself grew disillusioned when I found that none of the seven habits were ones I already had. Apparently Mr. Covey wanted me to learn *new* habits, which seems to be expecting quite a lot from me just because I bought his book.

I think the most productive people in the world belong to our parents' generation (Official motto: We don't want to be a burden). Whenever my in-laws come to visit, our house hums with activity. Casseroles are cooked. Bushes are trimmed. The driveway is edged.

Day after day they labor until the time comes for them to leave. As they pull out of the driveway, they look back with the tear-stained smiles of freed slaves, while my wife and I run along behind crying, "Please don't go. We've forgotten how to clean up after ourselves. Please; we'll buy you your own television."

People like this can't help being productive. You visit them in the hospital and they whisper, "If you bring me some Windex, I'll clean these windows."

I'm trying to be useful, but it doesn't come naturally. Like the time I was helping a friend move. It seemed like a positive thing to do until I banged her antique dresser into a rock wall. "Let's look on the bright side," I said. "The distressed wood look is very popular now."

Jesus knew the secret of a really useful life: "I am the vine," He said; "you are the branches. Those who remain in me, and I in them, will produce much fruit. For apart from me you can do nothing." (John 15:5, NLT).

He seems to be saying that if you think you're living a useful life without Him, it's a sham.

Let Me Put You on Hold
While I Turn the Other Cheek

Sometimes I wish the Bible were more specific. For example, I started looking for some counsel to "share" with my wife regarding how much money she can spend on a visit to the hair salon. The Bible writers are strangely silent on this subject. Is $100 too much? $200? Or is any amount all right as long as you make a matching contribution to Perms for the Poor?

If the prophets had been a little more specific, perhaps we would know how to deal with modern questions such as "Is it OK to clone a human being?" My answer is no, because too many of us would have our feelings hurt. Imagine one of your grown children saying, "Mom, we were thinking about cloning you for our next daughter, but we've decided to go with Katie Couric instead."

There's another contemporary issue that I wish had received the attention of the apostles, and that is the matter of what to do with telemarketers.

I get a lot of calls from these folks. I often pick up the phone to find a man with an inordinate interest in my septic system. Or it might be a woman offering me a credit card with exciting new benefits, including the ability to lower my cholesterol with every purchase.

I would like to stop these phone calls, but I don't know how. A quick exchange of e-mails with my senator informs me that there are legal issues that prevent the government from deporting telemarketers. It seems they are here to stay.

Of course, we could stop answering the phone, but there's always the chance that the caller will be a family member willing to talk about our health ailments. So what exactly should a Christian do when the person on the other end of the line cheerfully mispronounces our name and begins to extol the manifold wonders of their long-distance service?

The immediate temptation is to shout imprecations and slam down the phone. But I always have the nagging feeling that there's a little mark by my name on the telemarketing call sheet that says "Professed Christian."

What if the person calling mutters, "H'mmm. I can see that all that talk about brotherly love isn't cramping your style."

It helps to remember that telemarketers are not necessarily bad people. Just because they interrupt your supper does not make them evil on the same scale as a bioterrorist or a programming executive at MTV. Telemarketers are just doing their job—which, unfortunately, happens to be annoying. They're no worse than street mimes in that sense.

I have a kindly brother-in-law who believes that all telemarketers are unhappy in their job. So he views every sales call as a cry for help. Trying to be sympathetic, he will say, "Let's not talk business. I'd like to get to know you as a person." His conversations are generally very brief.

You can also keep your time on the phone to a minimum if you say, "I'll listen to your sales pitch if you'll listen to me describe the accomplishments of my granddaughter. She's in ballet, you know."

It's my belief that when Jesus was talking about turning the other cheek, He wasn't limiting his remarks to hand-to-hand combat. He meant for us to overlook petty annoyances that tempt us to unleash some annoying behavior of our own. It's times like this when we need to put someone on hold, and that someone is ourselves.

I'm Not Y40 Compliant

I'm getting older. This was brought to my attention when an anonymous friend left a birthday card on my desk, along with a brand-new denture brush. Very funny.

What kind of person would mock a friend on the eve of his 40th birthday? Just about every person, that's who. Apparently there is a bottomless barrel of mirth when it comes to the idea that people are becoming more wrinkled and closer to death.

Folks think it's funny that I am losing hair on my temples (while suddenly—out of nowhere—getting luxuriant growth from my ears). And they think it's a real hoot that I can't remember anything, including those three digits you're supposed to dial in an emergency. Well, we'll see how funny it is when they're lying on the floor with chest pains and the only phone number I know from memory is 1-800-Collect.

One of the differences between men and women—besides their level of interest in Richard Gere videos—is their reaction to growing older.

If you're a man, you tend to take each birthday stoically, suppressing feelings of failure that spring from the fact that Bill Gates owned a billion-dollar company when he was half your age, while your career has only now advanced to the point where the boss can call you by name without glancing at your name tag.

Women are more likely to welcome each birthday with peaceful serenity. The same peaceful serenity that they feel bungee jumping over a pit of spiders.

Why do women view the aging process with such fear and loathing? All I know is that little girls can't wait to hold up the number of fingers that indicate their age, but if you ask a big girl her age, she will target you with powerful eye beams that shrink you to the size of an Ingathering can.

Strangely enough, when a woman hits her eighth decade, she once again becomes eager to tell her age. I recently had Sabbath lunch with Aunt Nan, who steered the conversation—as she usually does—to the fact that she's 94 years old. If she had been a competitive woman, I might have wondered if it was her way of saying, "See if *you* can make it this far, punk."

Actually, I liked her attitude. I hate to see anyone lament growing older. Why should we feel bad about losing our youth? Youth is the time when getting a tattoo seemed like a good idea. And when the Fonz appeared to be the perfect life mate. And let me tell you, "Muskrat Love" by the Captain and Tennille was only great music to the young.

So we can live without youth. We will embrace maturity, enjoying the comfort of jeans with elastic waistbands and the emotional power of country music.

But we still really hate to give up strength and beauty. We don't want to lose our pep and to feel as though the warranty has run out on our bodies. We don't want to admit that we're using Lancome's double-performance treatment for "facial elasticity."

How desperately should we hold on to strength and beauty? I don't know, but it seems best to relax our grip. Isn't the whole exercise of faith letting go of what we once held so tightly, and waiting to see what God puts into our empty hands?

So here I am turning 40, and people are laughing at me.

I might as well join them.

Who's in Charge Here?

Friend, are you tired of people telling you what to do?

"I need that report on my desk in an hour," says your overbearing boss.

"You have to sew my costume for the school play," says your demanding child.

"Come back and see us again," says that pushy waitress at the Olive Garden.

Don't you think it's time *you* gave the orders? Well, I'm here to tell you how you can take charge of your life.

"But wait," I hear you saying. "How can I take control of my life? I can't even control my hair."

Ah, your hair. Let me direct your attention to a *real* product called Wella Liquid Hair Kryptonite.

Once you use this product, your hairdo will become as permanent as the Swiss Alps. I guarantee that bonding your hair so firmly in place that it cannot be affected by high winds or, for that matter, small-arms fire, will heighten your sense of control. The only downside is that if you decide to update your style, you need a professional stonemason.

Before we go any further, let me outline my qualifications for teaching you how to take control of a situation. I once was in total control of my life. I did what I wanted. I ate what I wanted. And I washed the dishes whenever I wanted. Sometimes I waited months to wash the dishes, and no one could do a thing about it (unless you count the time a government agency overreacted and put biohazard tape around my apartment).

Money was completely in my control. If I saw an urgent need to invest in shiny wheels for the car, I acted swiftly and decisively.

Basically, I called the shots. When I spoke, I spoke with the confidence of one who expected to be obeyed. "Give me a large order of fries," I said. And it was done.

It's hard to say when things began to change. As I look back, it seems that my sense of control began to wane at approximately the time I got married, give or take 45 minutes.

Then I discovered that my decision to have goulash for supper might be vetoed. Money I had set aside for the charitable purpose of entertaining the less fortunate with a home theater system might be squandered on beaded sandals.

So while marriage has many benefits—not the least of which is having someone handy to scratch between your shoulder blades—it does not enhance feelings of personal sovereignty.

And here's another thing. If you want to feel as though you're in control, make it your strict policy never to interact with small children. We have a 2-year-old in our house who is about as quick to obey our commands as a wild ferret. If we say "Come here," he just stares at us as if masked strangers are suggesting he carry their luggage on a cross-country flight.

Like other parents, we've fallen into the trap of trying to demonstrate our toddler's skills to others. "Show Aunt Paula how you answer the phone," we say. And nothing happens. We just get this look that seems to say, "If you want a performance, you *know* you need to talk to my agent."

OK, I admit that I'm not qualified to tell you how to gain control of any situation. But let me recommend the peace that comes from taking an out-of-control situation and putting it in the hands of the One who can command even the wind and the waves.

As for your hair—calming those waves will take a different kind of miracle.

Your Five-Minute Communication Seminar

Let's review the principles of good communication. "Wait!" I hear you saying. "I'm not interested in the principles of communication. I picked up this book so I could read jokes about your wife's shoes."

First of all, let me say that shoes are no laughing matter. They are a beautiful and indispensable part of civilized life. The next time you step into a public restroom at the Gas 'n' Go, remember that it is the noble shoe that places itself between you and the truly frightening forms of bacteria that are breeding on the floor. I am not ashamed to say that there have been times when footwear has caused my eyes to well up with tears. (Though that's usually when I see how much it adds to our Nordstrom bill.)

My primary point is that without communication, our relationships will fail and we will be left feeling very alone, much like a shopper at Kmart. So let's get to those important communication principles.

Principle 1: Timing is everything. Let's say you're at a gala awards dinner with your husband. If you notice that he has spinach on his teeth, he will appreciate your communicating that fact. But he will appreciate it even more if you tell him *before* he gets up to speak.

Principle 2: Clearly express your feelings. Women, when you communicate with the hairier sex, do not choose the path of subtlety and gentle suggestion.

My wife tried subtlety with me once. We were finishing up late at the office, and as we drove out of the parking lot, she asked what sounded to me—poor, ignorant fool—like a simple question. "Shall we skip going to the dry cleaner tonight?"

"Oh, I don't mind," I replied. "Might as well get it over with." Then I steered the family Honda in the direction of the dry-cleaning emporium.

Lori was shocked and offended. "Why are you going to the dry cleaner?" she demanded. She thought she had made it abundantly clear that she would rather be trapped in a cage full of badgers than go to the dry cleaner.

"Dear," I said, "next time you have a preference, why don't you hide it in an acrostic puzzle? Then I'll have a *chance* of figuring it out."

Principle 3: Use mirroring to become a better listener. Mirroring is where you repeat back to your partner what you think they are saying. This shows that you're paying attention—instead of thinking about a new hairstyle—and gives your partner a chance to correct any misunderstandings. Here's how it works:

Husband: "Please, oh, please, no. I'll do anything else. I'll put in that rock garden you want. I'll remove my unsightly nose hairs with a pair of pliers. Just please, please, don't make me go."

Wife: "I hear you saying that you don't want to take me antiquing."

Husband: "Thanks for understanding, dear."

Wife: "You're welcome. Get your keys."

Principle 4: Use "I" statements. When you express your feelings, you should always use "I" statements instead of "you" statements. "You" statements can sound judgmental.

Let's say you have a teenager who doesn't clean up their room. How should you approach the subject?

Wrong: "*You* never clean your room. *You* have totally ruined my chances of having our home featured in *Architectural Digest*."

Correct: "*I* feel like *I* would like to see your room cleaned up in 30 minutes, or *I* will take your car keys *and put* them someplace where you will never find them without taking SCUBA lessons."

⋆ ⋆ ⋆

OK, that's all we have time for today. But keep working on those communication skills. It's the best way we have to share truth, compassion, and love—all of which are beautiful and indispensable parts of civilized life.

Saving Pennies, Losing Sense

I hate goodbyes. Especially between me and my money. I guess you could call me a tightwad—though I prefer to think of myself as a "good steward."

I come from a family of Midwestern farmers whose regard for a dollar is similar to heaven's regard for lost souls: they rejoice when one is saved. You see, my aunts and uncles grew up in the Depression. To hear them tell it, they were so poor that if someone talked to them, they couldn't afford to pay attention.

It is often people who have lived through hard times to whom a dollar sticketh closer than a brother. Maybe that's why the Depression generation has spent the past 50 years saving for the *next* depression. This means they will leave huge sums of money for their kids, whose only memory of a depression is that sinking feeling they experienced when the Olive Garden ran out of raspberry truffle cheesecake. The kids will have the stash spent in a weekend.

However, my parents took precautions during my formative years to avoid this eventuality. They always acted like the Depression was still going on. For instance, my dad, an accountant, showed us how he ran his adding-machine tape through on both sides. And Mom saved grocery money by trying to pass off tomato soup as spaghetti sauce. Our happiest vacation memories involved getting 39 exposures out of a 36-exposure roll of film.

A penny saved was *better* than a penny earned. It was a copper-colored badge of honor.

When I moved out on my own, I continued to follow the pathway of cheapness. Top-floor apartments in rickety buildings without air conditioning. Homemade furniture. Lots of beans. I prided myself on living the ascetic life of a monk—only with more comparison shopping.

Then I married someone who didn't get as excited about saving money as I did. While I bought bulk shampoo by the gallon at Sam's Club. Lori lathered up from tiny vials of exotic shampoos that—judging by the

121

price—were extracted from glands of South American butterflies.

I tried to steer us to fast-food establishments, but she headed toward sit-down restaurants where—this is almost too painful to describe—I would have to pay a tip.

To me, saving money demonstrated character. So I saw the loosening of the wallet clasp as a lowering of standards. Would we become like those Philistines who ripped through paper towels to soak up kitchen spills, paid for full service at the gas pumps, and hung Dixie cup dispensers in their bathrooms?

No. I couldn't allow this to go on. So the next time she wanted to spend a little extra money on something, I came down on her like Moses from Mount Sinai. She had just picked up the most expensive jar of mayonnaise on the grocery store shelf.

I raised my voice in rebuke. "Look at this other stuff," I pointed. "It's also white and fluffy, and it's much cheaper."

"The same could be said of soap scum," she replied.

I tried to argue back, but it's hard to find a proof text on the merits of buying cheap mayo. Cheapskates such as myself may feel self-righteous in our dedication to saving, but we don't have much theological ground to stand on. In fact, the only person who mentions anything in the Bible about saving money is Judas.

So I've started to relax my grip on George, Abe, and Andrew. I have even gotten to the place where I've stopped washing and reusing aluminum foil. And I let Lori buy new shoes without moping around the house in sackcloth and ashes, prophesying our economic doom. Money is less important than relationships.

I should have paid more attention to my ancestors. They taught me how to save, but they also set an example of being generous with those around them.

This is what I have seen in the church. The same people who wouldn't think of buying anything for themselves unless it is on sale will dig deep in their pockets for the sake of their church school or local evangelism or the member who is laid off from work. This is storing up treasure in heaven, which—as we all know—is the best savings plan.

All We, Like Money, Have Gone Astray

There was no money in the Garden of Eden. Which was fine, because Adam would have been stumped for a place to keep a wallet.

Even after leaving their garden home, Adam and Eve never got around to inventing money. They were too busy scratching a living out of the hard earth and dealing with complaints that their family held too many church offices.

So the ancient world spun along without currency for quite some time. I'm guessing that a need for money finally surfaced at an ancient academy reunion. Classmates had no way to tell who had become the most successful. "If only there was some way to keep score," mused one alumnus who had made a name for himself in the mud-hut construction industry.

"I know," suggested a friend who was a rising star in the world of cave art. "Why don't we see who has the most sheep?"

It sounded like a good idea, and so after some brief—but intense—lobbying by the goat industry, it was decided that sheep would be the measure of wealth and success.

Sheep functioned like money in most ways. You could exchange them for goods and services. They were easy to count. And they tended to wander off and get lost about the time your tent mortgage was due.

In the old world, the shepherd served as both banker and stockbroker. He was like a banker in that he was supposed to keep your wealth safe. And he was like a stockbroker in that he was forever blaming the fact that you had less sheep than you did yesterday on the bear market.

The only difficulty with sheep was their size. On the one hand, they wouldn't get lost under the sofa cushions as modern coins do. But when you wanted to take a trip, they tended to slow you down a lot more than a pack of traveler's checks.

So men began to look for a more compact kind of currency, and their attention was drawn to bright, shiny objects such as gold and gems. (Even today men are attracted to shiny objects, such as drop-forged wrenches and new pickups.)

Gold and gems became a big hit as money. However, people felt insecure about leaving piles of the stuff lying around the house. So they came up with the idea of wrapping it around a woman's neck and arms and ankles. And that's how the ancients invented jewelry—little realizing the headache they had created for future Adventist youth workers.

Later, men came up with coins so that they wouldn't have to go get their wife and talk her out of a bracelet every time they wanted to buy something. Coins remained popular for thousands of years, partly because of the satisfying sound they make when you drop them in an offering plate.

Then things got so expensive that it took 10 pounds of coins to buy groceries, so people began to depend on banknotes. Basically this amounts to the government giving everyone bits of green paper and telling them to pretend it's worth something.

But paper money works. And it works better than sheep. For one thing, it's far less problematic when it comes to making change.

However, we miss out on one thing when we have a checking account instead of a woolly flock. We have less of an understanding of what God means when He says we are "the sheep of His pasture."

He is saying that even though we are silly and confused and unable to care for ourselves, we are as valuable to Him as money in the bank.

Finger Foods, Fainting, and Fire:
What Guys Love About Weddings

The Adventists I know are not extravagant people. It was not a church pioneer who coined the phrase "Keep the change." And have you noticed that when Sotheby's auctions a painting for $40 million, the buyer is never somebody you went to academy with?

However, there is one time when we allow ourselves to be extravagant. No, I'm not referring to the price we pay for FriChik. I'm talking about weddings.

Suddenly, the same people who consider it excessive to buy a name-brand breakfast cereal are ordering up caterers, tuxedos, and those guest-book pens with a feather on top. You might expect the church finance committee to approach the couple and point out that for the cost of their wedding they could repave the church parking lot.

But no one says anything. In matters of love, practical people know they must yield to extravagance.

Frankly, the whole wedding ceremony seems unnecessary to guys. Especially when we find out we have to dress up funny, stand in front of a crowd, and memorize complicated lines such as "I do."

That's why, about the time the bride is discussing the number of tiers for the wedding cake, the groom will drop a hint about eloping. To him, eloping seems quicker, cheaper, and less likely to interfere with Sunday afternoon sports on TV. A truly open-minded bride will consider the suggestion for about two seconds before finding a sweet way to say, "Shut up and stand on that piece of tape."

In the country of Kuwait, they have the consideration not to invite men to a wedding—except for a quick appearance by the groom. We might as well adopt this practice in the West, where the groom and his attendants don't have anything to do except serve as tuxedo wallpaper.

This is hard on guys because we like to *do* stuff, and the only job around is rolling out that little paper runner. That's why during the ceremony some grooms look like missionaries participating in a native folk dance—trying to be a good sport, but wishing they were working on the Land Rover.

Let me make it clear that men are not blind to the happily-ever-after romance of marriage. It's just that when we think of romance, we do not think of people marching around to classical organ music.

When men plan a wedding, you can tell the difference. Usually their program involves action and a threat to personal safety. When a couple says their vows while skydiving, you can be sure it wasn't the bride's idea to leap out of a Cessna in full-length wedding dress.

Speaking of danger, I once met a man who asked to get married just before going in to heart surgery. The medical staff put on a nice little ceremony in the hospital chapel, and this couple is the only one I know that has a cardiac monitor strip as a souvenir of their honeymoon night.

There's no denying that danger adds entertainment value to a wedding. That's why men appreciate bridesmaids like Shona McDermott, who added a considerable amount of excitement to a ceremony when her hair caught on fire. Apparently she had exceeded the legal limit for hair spray, and when she stood too close to the candelabra, *poof,* she was a human tiki torch. She suffered no injuries thanks to her 10-year-old son, who started beating her over the head with a pillow.

The promise of a disaster gives men a reason to go to weddings besides the finger foods. We had a good turnout at our nuptials because word had gotten around that Lori had fainted twice while getting fitted for her gown, so chances looked good for her to take a dive during the service.

We didn't have smelling salts, so the bridesmaids stashed vials of a powerful perfume in their bouquets. One whiff, and it felt like General Schwarzkopf was invading your sinuses. Anyway, to the vast disappointment of the audience, Lori finished the event in the upright position.

Yeah, I was the practical-headed guy at our wedding. Except for one single moment when the extravagance made sense to me. That was when I looked toward the end of the aisle and saw my bride, all beautiful and sparkling and smiling so brightly it made tears come to my eyes.

Isaiah says, "As a bridegroom rejoices over his bride, so will your God rejoice over you."* His love defies practical explanation. It is mysterious. It is astounding.

And yes, it is very, very extravagant.

---

*Isaiah 62:5

Your Life Will Never Be the Same

Y our life will never be the same," people said when Lori was pregnant. And they said it in an ominous way—like an Old Testament prophecy that involved pestilence and the sword.

They said it again and again, so I knew it must be true. Change was coming, and I couldn't avoid it any more than I could avoid death, taxes, and the Britney Spears publicity machine.

I was already apprehensive about parenthood. I mean, why would a rational person take on the responsibility of having a child? You can't find people to help with Vacation Bible School, and that requires that you put up with the ankle-biters for only one week. But parenthood is a 20-*year* commitment! More if your child is a music major.

On the other hand, I've never met anyone who regretted having kids. No one has ever come up to me and said, "You know, if I had it to do over again, we would have skipped having kids and put more time into our Shaklee vitamin business."

So I knew I was in for a change. But what kind of change? The best answer came in an e-mail from Matt Pierce, the father of two absurdly adorable girls named Sara and Sophia. Here's what he said:

Well, now that you're expecting, I can share with you the cold, hard facts. The reason they don't tell you about the cold, hard facts is because if you knew them, the human race would wither away into extinction. So here they are, summarized for your convenience.

1. You are no longer the center of the universe. Actually, consider yourself a fringe planet somewhere in the Gamma Quadrant. And in another 30 years you'll be considered a gaseous anomaly. At least that's how we see my father-in-law.

2. You no longer know anything. All the laws of nature are tossed on the floor like so much oatmeal.

a. Night is day and day is night; you'll learn to take little naps anywhere and anytime.

b. Water (and other fluids) will flow opposite their natural course. What should

127

go north to south in the child goes south to north. Later, you'll have the same problem with your household plumbing (Hint: It's probably Legos or marbles).

If you want to know more about this category, please refer to the plagues of Revelation 16. Incidentally, I think it's significant that the books Child Guidance and The Great Controversy were written at the same time.

3. You no longer have the luxury of having aversions to bodily fluids of any kind. I bet you didn't know it was a luxury . . . well, it WAS.

4. You will learn to embrace public television. The Teletubbies are: Tinky Winky, Dipsiy, Laa-Laa, and my favorite, Po. You will learn the Barney song; it comes in handy while cleaning. Elmo is the little furry red guy, and Baby Bear has some deep, dark side that I can't put my finger on. Mark my words, he's gonna go OFF and bust-a-cap on some Muppet one day.

Those are a few of the cold, hard facts. I have only one piece of advice for dealing with the pressure—blame the baby. When Lori is wondering who ate all the Special K loaf, blame the baby. When you want to leave an annoying social gathering, blame the baby. When you're late for work, blame the baby. The Greek word for baby and scapegoat are very similar.

So now that I've given you the cold, hard facts, what I really want to say is congratulations!

Your life will never be the same. And you'll be glad.

Life Was Simpler Then

W e took the baby to church for the first time last week because, frankly, we just wanted the attention.

The saints did not disappoint. They made a big fuss over him. However, I didn't appreciate their exclamations of relief that the child doesn't look like me. Often people would add a comment such as "It's good he'll have a chance at a normal life," or simply "We serve a merciful God."

Another interesting comment came from a friend, who said, "Wouldn't it be great to be a baby, without a care in the world?" Well, I had to give that some thought.

A baby's life is definitely simpler. For one thing, our boy doesn't have to worry about what to wear. That was decided for him by the women at the baby shower. Yes, there was some competition between the faction that likes choo-choo trains on clothes and the group advocating zoo animals. But overall, it's worked out pretty well.

In fact, this is such a great idea that many men follow the same policy throughout their entire adult lives—only wearing clothes brought to them by kindly women. They give their wives and mothers power of attorney over their wardrobe. (This is proof that men consider clothes shopping to have about the same entertainment value as chemotherapy.)

Women, let me remind you that your authority over what men wear is a sacred trust. Do not abuse it. Even if you think it would be a gigglefest to send your man off to his big meeting in a sailor suit and short pants, try to restrain yourself.

Here's another thing babies don't have to worry about–manners. When you're a baby, people *want* you to burp. And babies get a free pass to drool. Our kid drools so much that certain parts of the house qualify for federal flood relief, and nobody seems to care.

But the rules change completely for adults. If you saw your airline pilot with six inches of drool hanging from his lip, you'd be grabbing your carry-on bag and shouting, "GET THE BEVERAGE CART OUT OF

MY WAY. I'M TAKING THE BUS."

Yeah, a baby's approach to life is the essence of simplicity. If a baby had a Day-Timer, the appointment schedule would read: "Sleep. Eat. Relieve internal pressure. Repeat."

On those occasions when they leave the house, babies don't worry about finding a clean restroom or a restaurant that serves vegetarian food. They show no concern when they have a bad-hair day, nor do they trouble family members with questions such as, "Does this outfit make my thighs look fat?"

Once we humans grow up, life becomes more complicated. We have to deal with Internet viruses, dessert forks, and the expiration dates on yogurt. But as anyone who has studied the system for scoring Olympic figure skating can tell you, life is complicated because we make it that way.

I think that if Jesus had wanted our lives to be complicated, He would not have suggested that we become like little children. To quote Ellen White: "The simplicity, the self-forgetfulness, and the confiding love of a little child are the attributes that Heaven values. These are the characteristics of real greatness."★

So I'm trying to simplify my life. By the way, if any of you missed my baby shower back in 1958, I could use some new shirts.

★ *The Desire of Ages,* p. 437

What's That in Your Mouth?

I have heard people remark that small children are smarter than they seem. As the father of a 9-month old, all I can say is "I certainly hope so."

We love our child dearly, but—how can I put this kindly?—I'm not seeing any pressing need to set up a college fund. For one thing, he seems unable to tell the difference between real food and objects that have no nutritional value.

He has made serious efforts to eat a 749-page copy of *Les Misérables*, a throw rug, an aluminum chair, and a $20 traveler's check. Given the choice between eating the latest copy of *National Geographic* and a Gerber's product that is the exact same shade of yellow, he will choose the *National Geographic* every time.

They say that toddlers grow out of this stage, but don't bet on it. My friend Melynie has a 4-year-old daughter whom I shall call "Sally" in order to avoid any unpleasantness when she is old enough to hire a lawyer. On a trip to the beach this past summer, Melynie and Sally discovered a shop that offered "free" hermit crabs.

Now these crustaceans were free in the same sense that the elections in Zimbabwe are free. Melynie had to buy hermit crab food, a hermit crab cage, and probably hermit crab medical insurance.

Let us skip forward to the family's return from vacation. Sally wants to get to know her pet better, so she tries putting the seashell in her mouth. It just fits.

Then she sticks her tongue into the open end of the shell. The hermit crab does not recognize this as a gesture of friendship and grabs Sally's tongue with its big claw. Pandemonium ensues. Sally starts calling for her mother, though her enunciation is severely hampered.

"MRAUGH! HHHMM! NNNAAGH!"

After several seconds of confusion, Melynie looks into her daughter's mouth and finds the two-inch crab shell.

Her first reaction is to ask "Where's the video camera?" But she quickly realizes that Sally would not appreciate a delay for any purpose—even if the broadcast rights could pay off the mortgage. So Melynie instructs Sally to dangle her tongue (with the attached shell) under a water faucet until the crab releases its hold.

Like any good mother, Melynie blames herself. "It never occurred to me to warn my children not to stick their tongues into hermit crab shells."

I know it's not fair to make fun of what kids put in their mouths, especially when even adults can be careless in this area. I myself had a bite of potluck casserole in 1985 that haunts me to this day.

The other evening I was looking at a menu that listed "grilled baby octopus." I wanted to find someone who had ordered this particular appetizer, look into their eyes, and ask them, "Why?"

Perhaps there are people in the world who have nothing else to eat. But American grocery stores feature 50 different kinds of spaghetti sauce. The situation is not so desperate that we have to go rooting around for slimy, bottom-dwelling invertebrates. Besides, I'm sure you can get the same taste from boiled okra.

Now would be a good time to make some pronouncements about the importance of eating right. But I won't. First of all, I would have no credibility, because my own son would be delighted to eat an octopus if it ever came within reach. And second of all, Jesus said it isn't what we put *in* our mouths that makes us unclean; it's what comes *out* of them.

He's right, of course. Whatever the health effects of eating a bacon double cheeseburger, there is more to regret from speaking hurtful words to a friend or family member. Those are the times that it would be better if, just for a little while, a crab got our tongue.

The Adventures of Danger Dad

I assume it was a woman who said, "If they can send a man to the moon, why can't they send them all?" Frankly, I'm appalled by this attitude. Men serve a necessary function in society. They are the mafia lawyers, the heavyweight boxing champions, the CIA operatives, and the telemarketers that make this nation . . . well, never mind.

The important thing to remember is that men are the king of the home. Actually, "king" is more of an honorary title. It's like being the King of Sweden, whose main functions are inspecting the royal yacht and adjusting the castle thermostat.

Of course, men also have a role to play in providing for and protecting the children—though my wife isn't so sure about the protecting part. This stems from an incident in which I was supposed to be watching our 2-year-old at a friend's house.

All was well until the little tyke gave me the slip while I was in the kitchen looking for brownies. The next time my wife saw her only child, he was running back and forth in front of a flimsy screen door that opened onto the back deck. Which would have been fine except that the back deck had apparently left on a short vacation, leaving a nine-foot drop to concrete that reminded Lori of the view from the top of Hoover Dam.

Thanks to a good lawyer, I was able to reduce the charges from attempted murder to reckless endangerment.

Then there was the incident with the killer bees. The boy and I were playing in a park when Reef asked if he could investigate a plastic cup that sat on the ground.

"Sure, why not?" I said.

This was my first mistake. You see, my wife believes that litter is left behind not by ordinary, careless people but by patients in advanced stages of anthrax who summoned their last reserves of strength to escape their hospital room and order a Big Gulp at the 7-Eleven.

So this empty cup may have been teaming with germs that had the power to lay waste to our civilization. Only we'll never know, because as my son made his way to pick it up, a woman at a nearby house shouted for him to stop. She had used the cup to block the entrance to an underground hive full of angry, vicious bees. She had been stung numerous times, adding that it was the most horrifying experience in her life except for driving in New York traffic.

It is incidents like these that help me understand the black widow spider. As you know, she has the habit of mating and then including her husband in the all-you-can-eat honeymoon brunch. It's not that she doesn't like the guy. They had some good times, and she'll always think of him when she hears a Celine Dion song. But guys just aren't careful enough with children. As she sees it, eating the father is a safety precaution.

Fortunately, my wife is willing to keep me around because she needs someone to mow the lawn. However, I have been placed on a kind of probation in which she checks on me every two minutes to make sure I'm not teaching our boy to juggle knives.

Actually, I don't know anyone who is fully competent to be a parent. We all make mistakes with our kids, some of which involve a need to call poison control and some of which will allow their future therapist to buy a new Lexus.

I wonder why God doesn't say, "Hey, we'll raise the kids in heaven, because you people goof up too much." But He gives us breathtaking responsibility along with our breathtaking freedom. It's a package deal.

So I'm trying to measure up to the responsibility. I really should put off teaching the boy to juggle with knives until next year.

Famous First Words

I've been flipping through *The Baby Book,* trying to find out if it is normal for a 16-month-old child to form a religion around a household appliance. Every morning and every evening, our son grabs my wife or myself by a finger and drags us to the closet where we keep our vacuum cleaner.

At first we thought he was encouraging us to clean the floor, which is hidden under a layer of stepped-on Cheerios. But then we noticed that he approaches our upright Hoover with an attitude of reverence and devotion that I most often associate with visitors to the holy sepulcher or callers on *The Rush Limbaugh Show.* I wonder if it's time to teach the boy about the first commandment.

During my reading I also stumbled across this alarming piece of information: According to *The Baby Book,* "The average baby may speak only four to six intelligible words by 15 months." This is alarming because it indicates that "average" babies are speaking a month before our son. I'm afraid that even when he's a teenager, he won't *ask* to borrow the car keys. He'll just grunt and point.

Now, I can hear some of you saying, "That *is* how my teenager asks to borrow the car keys."

Other more reassuring readers are saying, "Don't obsess over it. Your child will talk soon enough."

What you fail to understand is the pressure that we are under. You see, we go to church with the Hansons. We had always had a warm and non-competitive relationship with this couple—right up until the moment they mentioned that their granddaughter recited the Pledge of Allegiance at the tender age of 18 months. We went home that day and said, "Son, you have two months to learn Hamlet's soliloquy."

So far, it hasn't worked. In fact, we've failed so utterly in teaching our son to speak English that he has given up and is trying to teach us baby language.

The other morning we were reading a book about cats. He pointed to a picture of one of our feline friends and said, "Bap-umm." I said, "Cat." He pointed again and said, "Bap-umm." I replied, "No, it's a cat."

The child gave me a look that indicated he was trying hard to be patient with such a slow learner. He pointed again very insistently. "BAP-UMM!" Now when we read *The Cat in the Hat*, it doesn't have the same rhythm.

"Bap-umm" is a favorite word that can describe many things: a cat, a dog, the car, and—for all I know—certain aspects of particle physics.

Now, I should point out that both grandmothers hold the opinion that our son has already spoken. Such as the time his stroller came around the corner in Target and he saw a display of vacuum cleaners. "Bap-umm," he declared, and my mother was certain that he had said "vacuum." *No*, I thought, *that's Reef's word for cats and the second law of thermodynamics.*

At least that's what I used to think. Then this past week Reef dragged me to the closet, pointed at the Hoover, and said, "Bap-umm." That's when it dawned on me. "Vacuum" is his favorite word. Maybe he's been talking all the time, and I just haven't been listening.

One of the most difficult activities, next to opening the plastic wrapper on a new CD, is to really, truly listen. To our family. To our workmates. To God.

"Thou shalt have no other gods before me" is another way of saying, "Pay attention. Don't get distracted by trivial things."

Even if we're not obsessed with the wonders of a Hoover Elite Supreme, the human mind is always ready to get hung up on something else. Which reminds me. If we're going to beat this Hanson kid, we've got to find a sonnet or something that begins with "vacuum."

Yabba-Dabba Do Not

You look like you need a vacation. Or maybe you've just returned from one. It's hard to tell the difference between a person in need of rest and a person who has spent a week in a minivan with two kids and a Tickle Me Elmo.

I have heard of people who know how to relax on their days off. They go to the beach with a large book and refuse to move unless (a) a child limps in from the waves with a shark clamped to their ankle, or (b) they need more suntan lotion.

I respect this approach to vacation. However, it is not the way I was raised as a child. When my family went on vacation, we moved with the speed and purpose of Army reconnaissance. We once viewed all the sights from Washington, D.C., to Boston in one week. "Hurry," my dad would say. "Run in there and see the Liberty Bell, then get back out. Don't fool around and read the placards like you did at the Smithsonian. It's a big bell with a crack in it. That's all you need to know. I'll leave the engine running."

The engine was *always* running. When we hit New York City, we flew through town like a Bill Clinton book tour. My brother sneezed and missed the Empire State Building completely.

Our folks wanted us to see as much of the world as possible—but they did not want us to see what was on television. This was disappointing to a couple of kids who would much rather watch one episode of *The Flintstones* than view Plymouth Rock. And there was another problem. The lack of advertising exposure left us confused about which breakfast cereals we should crave. Once we actually ate homemade granola without complaining.

I think my parents were afraid we would see something on television that would leave us warped. Maybe it could happen. But it's hard to believe that people have been set on a life of crime by watching *Gilligan's Island*. Unless, maybe, it was a series crimes involving coconuts.

It all comes down to the saying "Monkey see, monkey do." That's why parents get concerned about TV in general and *The Osbournes* in particular. My message of comfort to them is this: Think about how many times your children have seen you wash the dishes. Have you ever surprised them in the kitchen imitating that behavior? Exactly.

Of course, that's my argument when I'm talking about *your* kids. When it comes to *our* kid, my wife and I have limited his video experience to a single *Baby Mozart* tape. We figure it's safe because it is excruciatingly boring. It's the entertainment equivalent of being stuck in an elevator. The plot centers around the numbers 1 through 9 and footage of the producer's dog. It is so dull that sometimes I'm distracted from the television screen by the sensation of my fingernails growing.

The problem of what to watch is a modern one. Go back 100 years, and you wouldn't have much to look at besides the back of a mule team. You didn't agonize over whether to watch a show in which people eat spiders or a show in which the stars chat it up around the autopsy table.

I suppose that being careful about what you watch is similar to being careful about what you eat. You're better off, even though it's hard to prove that it has saved your life. So I'll suggest a wholesome, balanced diet for the eyes. Go on vacation and see Yosemite, the *Louvre*, and sunsets at the beach. And maybe, every once in a while, you can watch *The Flintstones* for dessert.

A Prescription
From Dr. Feelgood

My 3-year-old son gives me a lot to think about. Sometimes he makes me think, *How much should I tip the waiter to deal with this mess?* Or he makes me think, *How does he break something like that with his bare hands?*

Of course, there are times when he makes me think, *Ah, what an adorable kid!* And there are other times when I think, *Either this boy really needs a nap, or we should call an exorcist.*

But he definitely gave me food for thought when he started making up his own prayers. One of his first prayers was "Dear Jesus, help me to feel good. Amen."

Now, I should point out that this was not a prayer of despair from a heart heavy with the burdens of the world. Did I mention that Reef is 3 years old? He has no credit card debt. No work stress. No problems with his prostate. He has more toy cars than Kmart. Frankly, he would never be sad at all if his mom would let him have more candy.

So I'm not sure why, but he said he wants to feel good.

Don't we all? We want to feel good about our careers, our parenting skills, and our azaleas. A whole industry has grown up around our need to feel good about our fingernails.

So why don't we hear this kind of prayer more often? Why doesn't the first elder get up in church and pray, "Lord, some of us are depressed about our age and nervous about the stock market. Some of us have back pain, and, personally, those huevos rancheros I had this morning aren't sitting too well. Help us to feel good."

Our desire to feel good governs everything we do from the time we get up until we clean the lint from between our toes at bedtime. But we don't like to admit it. There are parts of New England where a person won't talk about how he feels even if he steps in a bear trap.

Of course, I'm talking about men. Women are more willing to describe their feelings. Often I hear a woman saying something like, "I feel bad about bringing this wedding present. I wanted the wrapping paper to match the bridesmaids' dresses." And all her friends have to gather around and assure her that the wrapping paper really is lovely and that there is no cause for tears.

Which makes me think that there is no telling what people will feel bad about. And feeling good is not always evidence that everything is in a state of goodness.

In fact, I was relieved when Reef gave up the "feel good" prayer and started making more specific petitions. One time he prayed, "Dear Jesus, please help me not to get stains on my shirts when I eat." *That's right, son, I thought to myself, and while you're asking for miracles, why don't you ask for an end to war and poverty?*

But I had to admit that it was an improvement. It is better when our prayers are more concerned with being good than with feeling good. If you're being good, feeling good seems to follow. And not the other way around.

Kinda makes you think, doesn't it?

The Sugar-Driven Life

T*he Purpose-Driven Life,* by Pastor Rick Warren, has sold 24 million copies. That's a lot of books and probably explains why the employee benefits at Zondervan now include a free polo pony.

Why was this book so successful? I think it's because we all crave a sense of purpose.

Our ancestors had plenty of purpose. Their goal was to get through the day without being eaten by wolves. But modern life is different. You can go all week without realizing a higher purpose than finding a cheap gas station.

I admit that some people have noble purposes. They wake up in the morning with the goal of rescuing people from burning buildings, or putting a stop to global warming, or beating back the plague of toenail fungus. But the rest of us are absorbed in ventures such as getting the cellophane wrapper off of our new Yanni CD.

It's hard to feel that you're fulfilling a special destiny when your biggest accomplishments of the day include putting new staples in the stapler and flossing.

That's why I envy my son, Reef, who's now 4. He has a passion and a purpose. That purpose is the pursuit of sugar. The sound of opening a package of cookies can bring the boy running from the farthest reaches of the house. If someone offers him a piece of candy, he stands up as if a choir has begun the "Hallelujah Chorus."

The other day Reef was at the point of tears because he had been denied a new toy. He looked up with the big liquid eyes you normally see painted on a Precious Moments figurine and asked, "Can I have a cookie to comfort me in my sadness?"

Who doesn't like cookies? I'm thinking of my friend Bill, who came home to see a tray of freshly baked cookies. Some had a thick layer of frosting. Others had very little. He had picked up one with a thin layer of frosting when his grandson stopped him. "You can't eat the ones without frosting—they're for Cameron," said the grandson, referring to his little brother.

"Oh, yeah?" replied Bill, popping the cookie into his mouth. He was the head of household. He would decide which cookies to eat. Bill was soon informed that the reason certain cookies were reserved for Cameron was that the 2-year-old had licked the majority of the frosting off of them.

Frosting holds such a powerful attraction for children that most of them would probably try to lick it off a porcupine.

Yet as his parents, we try to rein in Reef's sweet tooth because we've heard that sugar is the least healthy foodstuff next to deep-fried nuclear waste. On the other hand, we are not blind to the fact that sugar is a powerful motivating force when used as a treat. I believe that if we gave the boy a small shovel and used a large package of M&M's in a judicious way, we could get him to dig an inground swimming pool.

Sugar has been a motivating force since its discovery by the great explorer Captain Crunch. But it's not the only one. I suppose the time will come when my son will move beyond his interest in sugar and become obsessed with go-karts. Then in a few more years it will be female companionship. And a few years after that he will be focused on finding a good fiber supplement.

Our goals come and go. I remember those times when I purposed in my heart to start a vigorous exercise program. Those moments were immediately followed by a purposeful trip to see what was in the refrigerator. I learned that if you want to start an exercise program, you need a partner who will motivate you to stick with it. Preferably a marine drill sergeant.

If our attention is always wandering, where can we get a real sense of purpose? The apostle Paul has an answer. He says, "It is God who works in you to will and to act according to his good purpose."*

To me, that means that if I let Him, God will fulfill a purpose in my life that is more sublime and more lofty than any of the goals that I can come up with on my own. Sweet, huh?

---

*Philippians 2:13

Bunnies, Pirates,
and a Child's Prayers

My son, Reef, who's just turned 5, gets a lot of prayers answered. It's not to the point where the neighbors are bringing by the sick and infirm, but he's had a pretty good run lately. The other day I watched him dash around the house in search of an oversized stuffed bunny until he suddenly remembered the power of prayer. He went from a dead run to the praying position so fast that he actually skidded across the wood floor on his knees.

"Dear Jesus," he said, "please help me find my pink bunny. Please, please, please."

The next time you pray for world peace, trying saying "please" three times because it worked for Reef. A few minutes later he found his bunny.

He's getting used to having his prayers answered, which makes me nervous. Will he be disillusioned if heaven doesn't rally around to his next request? I mean, the old bedtime stories don't prepare a kid for that kind of situation. They tend to focus on the time little Harry prayed and found his boat, not the time his toy became an aquarium decoration at the bottom of a pond.

I guess we don't want to send youngsters the message that "God *sometimes* answers prayer." We're afraid that no child will jump into the baptismal tank after that kind of advertising. Today, people want guarantees. So we think we need to tell them that God will answer all prayers—or their offerings will be cheerfully refunded.

Of course, many people believe that God *does* answer every prayer. They contend that He sometimes says "yes," He sometimes says "no," and He sometimes says "Have you thought about putting a hook for your car keys by the door?"

I don't think children are heartbroken by a "no" answer. Goodness knows that they've heard plenty of "no's" from parents. "No, you may not hot glue your sister's hair to the wall!" we say with some energy. "No, you can't test your paper-towel parachute on the cat!"

If we think about it, we don't even *want* our every prayer answered with a "yes." Remember when you were living in that house with a yard the size of a welcome mat and your daughter was praying for a pony? That answered prayer would definitely have resulted in a stern letter from the homeowners' association.

We shouldn't expect a positive answer to all our prayers because, frankly, we don't even know what it involves. It's like tugging on the steering wheel that drives the universe. Maybe the tug will result in some gain for us—but who can count the cost to someone else. To divert the flow of nature may have some price in the great war between Christ and Satan that we don't yet see.

My boy is going to face a "no" answer fairly soon. I just heard him pray to Jesus, "Help us to find a treasure box with lots of jewels." Say what you want about my faith, but I don't think it's going to happen. My guess is that God is not going to encourage the current pirate craze because, well, He remembers pirates.

Yesterday I was trying to find a lost power tool. As I pursued my search from room to room, I heard Reef call after me, "I prayed to Jesus that you would find your drill."

Sure enough, I found it. I told Reef about his answered prayer and observed that "God is good to us."

"He sure is," replied Reef with enthusiasm.

Will God still be good if Reef doesn't get his treasure chest? Will He still be good even if we perceive no response to our more serious supplications? The answer, in this case, is always "yes."